Maureen Hunter
THREE PLAYS

THREE PLAYS
Maureen Hunter

Footprints ON THE Moon
Beautiful Lake Winnipeg
Transit OF Venus

Maureen Hunter: Three Plays
first published 2003 by
Scirocco Drama
An imprint of J. Gordon Shillingford Publishing Inc.
©2003 Maureen Hunter

Footprints on the Moon, Beautiful Lake Winnipeg and *Transit of Venus* were originally published by Blizzard Publishing in 1988, 1990 and 1992 respectively.

Scirocco Drama Series Editor: Glenda MacFarlane
Cover Design by Doowah Design Inc.
Author photo by Earl Kennedy
Printed and bound in Canada

Published with the financial assistance of The Canada Council for the Arts and the Manitoba Arts Council.

Production inquiries (except Britain and Europe) should be addressed to:
Patricia Ney, Christopher Banks and Associates
6 Adelaide Street, Suite 610
Toronto, Ontario, Canada M5C 1H6
416-214-1155
cbanks@pathcom.com
Production inquiries for Britain and Europe should be addressed to:
M. Steinberg Playwrights
104 Great Portland Street
London, England W1W 6P3
020-7631-1310
Micheline@SteinPlays.com

Canadian Cataloguing in Publication Data

Hunter, Maureen, 1947–
    Three plays/Maureen Hunter.
Contents: Footprints on the moon—Beautiful Lake Winnipeg—Transit of Venus.
ISBN 1-896239-99-8
    I. Title.
PS8565.U5814T47 2003   C812'.54   C2003-901482-7
PR9199.3.H828T47 2003

J. Gordon Shillingford Publishing
P.O. Box 86, RPO Corydon Avenue, Winnipeg, MB Canada R3M 3S3

Table of Contents

Maureen Hunter

Maureen Hunter is one of Canada's most successful playwrights. Her work has been produced extensively on Canada's major stages, in the United States and Britain and by CBC and BBC Radio. Her play *Transit of Venus*, premiered by Manitoba Theatre Centre, has received a string of successful productions and became the first Canadian play ever staged by the Royal Shakespeare Company of Britain. Other plays include *Vinci* (Scirocco, 2002), *Atlantis* (Scirocco, 1997, a finalist for the Governor General's Award), *The Queen of Queen Street* (Nuage Editions, 1997), and a play for young audiences, *I Met a Bully on the Hill*, co-authored with Martha Brooks (Scirocco, 1995). A native of Saskatchewan, Maureen now lives on the banks of the Red River in Winnipeg.

Preface

Between 1983, when I started writing plays, and 1992, when *Transit of Venus* premiered on the mainstage at Manitoba Theatre Centre, I wrote five full-length plays. This collection contains three of them. The first, *Footprints on the Moon*, is set in a prairie town, a town resembling the one I knew growing up. The second, *Beautiful Lake Winnipeg*, is set on a remote shore of Lake Winnipeg, which I saw for the first time when I moved to Manitoba in 1971. *Transit of Venus* is set in eighteenth century France.

To the outsider, the similarities between these plays may seem tenuous. Not to me. I know the thread that connects them: my own sense of place, and the impact of place on story.

As a child growing up on a farm in southern Saskatchewan, it seemed to me there were two kinds of people in the world: those who stayed where they were raised and those who left. I sensed that I would fall into the second category—not without paying a price. The price of leaving, I came to understand, was loss. But there is loss involved in every decision we make. In a sense, our lives are shaped by loss—or, to put it more positively, by the growth we achieve through loss.

In search of a way to explore this subject, I stumbled on the character of Joanie. She first appeared in one of my short stories, "Summertime Man," published in *Prairie Fire* (Summer 1986). She grew into the Joanie we meet in *Footprints on the Moon*. Her story is a testament to the simple truth that losing is part of living, and that we can't allow our losses, no matter how profound, to diminish us. At the same time, she represents the hope I think we all nourish that something in our lives will endure...like the footprints on the moon.

The moment I laid eyes on Lake Winnipeg, I fell in love with it. It's more than a lake, it's a vast inland sea: beautiful, treacherous, inscrutable. It was only a matter of time before I found a story appropriate to the lake. That story is *Beautiful Lake Winnipeg*. I wrote it because I enjoy plays about adults playing games and I wanted to try my hand at one. I'm also partial to black humour and I'd been looking for a story that would support that kind of humour. I named it *Beautiful Lake Winnipeg* because I liked the irony of the title in the context of the play, and as a secret tribute to Gabrielle Roy, whose short story "The Old Man and the Child" concludes with those words.

The genesis of the play was a line that popped into my head: "So—you think you're going to marry my wife." From that line the play evolved. As it evolved, I learned something that surprised me: it's fun to work with amoral characters. Once you accept them for who they are, there are no limits to what they will say or do, except the limits imposed by your own courage and imagination.

Although *Transit of Venus* is set in the eighteenth century and far from the Canadian prairies, it has its genesis on the prairies too. A childhood on the prairies is a childhood spent under wide spectacular skies. At night, far from the city, the stars sometimes hang so low you feel as close to them as to the land at your feet. My fascination with the night sky led me in 1988 to enrol in a course in astronomy at the University of Winnipeg. It was during that course that I first heard of the transits of Venus, and of one French astronomer who paid, it seemed to me, an inordinate price for the pursuit of knowledge. Even before I knew his name, I was determined to write about him. The word "Venus" suggested a love story—but how, I wondered, could any woman compete with the lure of the sky, the call of the sea, the hunger for knowledge? That question shaped the play.

As the play evolved, I came to understand that while Le Gentil's quest was the most spectacular, all the characters were involved in quests. They were all striving to understand who they were in relation to one another, and to God. They were all learning about love, commitment, forgiveness, faith, loss, renewal—the same basic lessons we struggle with today.

Although *Transit of Venus* is technically the only historical play in this collection, I've come to think of *Footprints on the Moon* as an historical play too. The whistle of a train may still slice the prairie silence like a knife, but small town train stations like the one in Rose Coulee are gone. As for *Beautiful Lake Winnipeg*, the proliferation of cell phones has made the situation established in Act One a little more challenging to stage than when the play premiered in 1990.

It's sobering to consider how quickly this has happened, but I suppose it shouldn't be surprising. Every creation reflects a moment in time and space. If that moment resonates in other times and spaces, what more can we ask?

M.H., January, 2003

Footprints on the Moon

*This play is dedicated to the memory
of my mother, Stella Horsman*

Production Information

Footprints on the Moon was first produced by Agassiz Theatre Company on January 21, 1988, at the Gas Station Theatre, Winnipeg, with the following cast:

JOANIE .... Pam MacDonald
DUNC CARR .... Wayne Nicklas
CAROL-ANN .... Natasha Klassen
BERYL .... Sharel McCulloch
BOONE .... Jonathan Barrett

Directed by Craig Walls
Set design by David Hewlett
Lighting design by Dennis Smith
Stage management by Charlene Wiest
Artistic Director: Craig Walls
Executive Producer: Julianne Krause

Footprints on the Moon was workshopped at the 1986 Playwrights Colony sponsored by the Manitoba Association of Playwrights. The playwright is grateful to George Toles for his insight, criticism and encouragement during the writing of this play.

Setting

Rose Coulee, a prairie town, 1980s: the train station; Joanie's kitchen and porch.

Characters

Act One

Scene One

The train station. A hot Thursday afternoon in August. JOANIE enters carrying a paper bag and a vivid purse. She wears a sundress and high-heeled sandals; everything is a little too tight. She has just walked across town and is obviously hot and uncomfortable. She pulls the top of the sundress away from her body and fans her breast with the dress. She moves up centre and peers off left, shading her eyes, sighs, faces front, swats a mosquito. She removes one sandal, shakes something out of it, takes the other sandal off too. She moves to the station wall and leans against it. Realizing that the wall is cool, she presses one shoulder, then the other, against it. Then she slips to the ground and sits, her back against the wall, her legs straight out in front of her. She spreads her legs wide, raises the skirt of the dress and fans herself with it. A truck is heard drawing closer, turning in. Brakes; the engine is turned off.

JOANIE: Damn.

A truck door slams. JOANIE stands reluctantly and is putting her sandals back on when DUNC enters. He wears jeans, cowboy boots, a white shirt, a western-style hat and a wide leather belt with an ornate silver buckle. He's tanned, trim and very fit.

There's an awkward moment when they first see one another.

Well, if it isn't.

DUNC: Joanie.

           *DUNC moves up centre, peers left; he makes quite a
           show of checking things out.*

JOANIE: It's already been and gone.

DUNC: Sure it has.

JOANIE: It has.

DUNC: Then how come you're still here?

JOANIE: Maybe I enjoy the view.

DUNC: The view.

JOANIE: That one you are standing in front of.

           *DUNC draws a package of cigarettes from his shirt
           pocket, lights one, looks her over.*

DUNC: Who're you waitin' for, anyhow? In them fancy new
           clothes.

JOANIE: Carol-Ann. My daughter.

DUNC: I remember who she is. *(Turns to stare off.)* Well, she's
           late.

JOANIE: We don't need to ask who you've come for.

DUNC: What's that supposed to mean?

JOANIE: Just—we don't need to ask.

           *DUNC lets this pass. He takes off his hat, wipes an
           arm across his forehead.*

DUNC: God, this heat. Ain't it hot out here? Nothin' to sit on,
           either. You'd think they could've left a goddamned
           bench. To even get the train to stop, you hafta call
           three days ahead. Whole town's goin' downhill.

JOANIE: No, it's not.

DUNC: Sure as hell is.

JOANIE: What are you trying to do, make me mad?

DUNC: I'm givin' it my best shot. *(He grins.)*

JOANIE: It's not going downhill. It's just kind of—plateau'd.

DUNC: Yeah? That what you wrote in that Prize Winnin' Essay?

JOANIE: Not exactly.

DUNC: What'd you write?

JOANIE: You'll see. They're printing it Friday in *The News*. Maybe you'll remember to read it.

           JOANIE throws him a glance, then moves away.

DUNC: Kinda nice to see you, all dolled up. A dress and everything. I like to see a woman in a dress. You don't wear 'em much, do you? You mostly wear those short-shorts the boys all let on they never notice.

JOANIE: What boys?

DUNC: Over at the Plains Inn.

JOANIE: The Plains Inn! Why don't you call that place what it is?

DUNC: What is it?

JOANIE: It's a dirty old machine shed, that's what.

DUNC: *(Shrugs.)* Sour grapes.

JOANIE: Huh! Think I want to hang around a place like that?

DUNC: I think you wanna be where you'd get a few laughs.

           He knows this will make her smile. It does, but she catches herself.

JOANIE: I don't see why it has to be "No Women Allowed."

DUNC: Oh, there's a pretty good reason for that.

He grins broadly. JOANIE turns away.

So. Where's Carol-Ann been off to?

JOANIE: Ask me something you don't know.

            A direct hit. DUNC shifts, drops his cigarette, grinds it out, stares off.

DUNC: Old Boone. Sure gotta give him credit.

JOANIE: Do you?

DUNC: Well, I mean, he sends for her every summer, don't he? Just like clockwork. Pays her way, too, or no?

JOANIE: A real hero.

DUNC: Lots do worse.

JOANIE: What goes on in there, anyhow?

DUNC: Where?

JOANIE: All of a sudden there's not a man to be seen , they're all hiding out in that dirty old machine shed. What goes on?

DUNC: Nothin'.

JOANIE: Nothin'!

DUNC: Honest to God, nothin' goes on. Don't know why you women are all so upset about it. It's just a bunch of guys sittin' around. Shootin' the breeze, playin' a little poker. Tossin' back a few…

JOANIE: Sounds awful dull to me.

DUNC: Dull's the one thing it ain't.

JOANIE: *(Leaning up against the station wall.)* You're a born bachelor, I guess. What a stroke of luck for your Mum.

DUNC: I'd make one lousy husband, that's for sure.

JOANIE: They all say that.

DUNC: Who?

JOANIE: Any man with sense. Any man I ever knew. What are you staring at?

DUNC: How come you're all dolled up, anyhow?

JOANIE: Orders.

DUNC: Who's givin' you orders?

He moves close to her, sets one hand against the station.

Nobody gives you orders.

JOANIE: *(Moving away.)* Carol-Ann, that's who. "Don't bother meeting me," she says, "or if you've got to come, dress decent!" That's how it is with kids. You start out by giving orders and end up taking them.

DUNC: I guess.

JOANIE: "Leave the short-shorts at home," she says. That's what she learns in The Big T.O. That kind of talk. I can already see her face—the look on it, when she steps off that train. I bought her a present, to cheer her up.

She opens the paper bag, pulls out a woolen scarf and mitts.

Hand-knit mitts and a scarf to match! From the U.C. Tea and Bake Sale, last Saturday. I looked at blue, you know—sky blue? They would've matched her eyes perfect. But somehow or other I ended up with these. You haven't said yet how pretty they are.

DUNC: Well, they're pretty all right, but they're—wool aren't they?

JOANIE: *(Faltering.)* Well, sure. It was wool or aprons with matching pot holders—take your pick! Oh, maybe I shouldn't have got them, maybe I should save them for Christmas. *(Brightening.)* One thing about Carol-Ann, when you give her something she really cuts up. She's got what's called A Dramatic Personality, that's why. When she was little, she was always in front of the mirror—she's always in front of the mirror now. When she was little...

> *Realizing she has lost his interest, she sticks the scarf and mitts back in the bag.*

She'd cry her heart out over nothing, just to watch herself do it. I haven't seen her in three weeks.

DUNC: It's all right.

> *He draws a mickey from his pocket, uncaps it, offers it to her.*

JOANIE: I better not.

DUNC: Goes down real nice.

JOANIE: You know what happens when I drink it straight.

DUNC: *(Grins.)* Yeah—I do!

> *JOANIE gives him a look.*

Just a swallow.

> *JOANIE takes a drink, makes a face, hands the bottle back.*

JOANIE: How's your Mum doing, anyways? Better?

DUNC: Aw...you know.

JOANIE: That's too bad.

DUNC: She's got this new specialist now. Best in the west—supposed to be. *(Indicating the track.)* That's where she's been all week. She seems to think he's helpin'. Me, I don't see it. I just hope one thing. *(Meaning "dies in her sleep:")* Hope she sleeps out.

JOANIE: I hope so too.

DUNC: Listen here, Joanie. How come you kept it so quiet? Carol-Ann bein' out of town. I had no idea.

JOANIE: Well, how could you? Place the size of this.

DUNC: You should've advertised it. Raised a banner!

JOANIE: Anyone that mattered knew.

DUNC: Is that so?

JOANIE: Yes, it is.

DUNC leans into her.

DUNC: I don't think so.

JOANIE: You don't.

DUNC runs a finger along her arm.

DUNC: I don't.

JOANIE throws off his hand.

JOANIE: You never were no Rhode scholar. *(She moves away.)*

DUNC: Shit.

JOANIE: I didn't notice you letting it slip by last summer. Nor the summer before.

DUNC: All right, Joanie.

JOANIE: Every August like clockwork, you said it yourself.

DUNC: All right, have it your way! I knew, but I kept my distance. You wanna know why?

JOANIE: No! I know why.

DUNC moves upstage, stands with his back to her, staring off.

God, this weather. The air's so hot, it hums. I need to pee too. Where's a person supposed to pee, anyways? *(A smile grows.)* That Carol-Ann. When she was little she peed practically non-stop. Did I ever tell you that? She did. It wasn't her fault. She had this problem, something down there didn't work right, not 'till she was almost three. And one time— *(Laughs.)* One time Boone picked her up in her birthday suit and swung her across the table but not fast enough and she peed all over his Cream o' Wheat! She did. *(Beat.)* I notice you've still got that fender dent. How come?

DUNC: Haven't got around to fixin' it.

JOANIE: I thought maybe you'd kept it to remember me by.

DUNC: I don't need no fender dent for that.

JOANIE: You're a devil, Dunc Carr, you know that? Lies just flow off your tongue like rain off a roof.

DUNC: I mean it, Joanie.

JOANIE: That fender dent. It's no wonder you got it. By the time you got to my place, you were half the time so pie-eyed you could hardly get through the door.

DUNC: Once I did, I managed fine.

JOANIE: You sure did! And now from what I hear you're managing fine over at Jamieson's.

            Dead silence.

            From what I hear.

DUNC: You can't say I didn't warn you, Joanie.

JOANIE: Oh, well. You and half the town. *(Mimics.)* When a man comes calling at 2 a.m., it's for one thing only.

DUNC: Who'd say that?

JOANIE: Some of them were pals of yours.

DUNC: Jealous.

JOANIE: I wonder.

DUNC: I told you right at the start, I don't like to be counted on.

JOANIE: That'll be news to a few people around here. All the boys over at the Plains Inn—

DUNC: I don't like to be counted on by no woman!

JOANIE: I wonder if your Mum ever got that message?

DUNC: Are you going to pick on her? Now? As things stand?

JOANIE: No. I'm not.

             She moves away, fanning herself.

             I should've worn my shorts anyways. No matter what she said.

DUNC: It wasn't for one thing only!

JOANIE: She never used to talk like that, not Carol-Ann. She never used to order me around. He's done that, I guess—or Toronto. Or maybe I brought it on myself. I didn't always handle things so good, I know that. Starting right when she was three years old and crying, "Where is he, where'd he go, why-why-why!" I'd just always say the same thing. "Honey, all I know is this. He walked into the Drake Hotel one night and didn't bother coming out." What a mistake. She's never once gone by that damned hotel without staring at it like it was some kind of shrine! True. Enough to break your heart.

DUNC: You better come out of the sun, Joanie. Why don't you?

JOANIE: Dropped right out of sight for ten and a half years. But now he sends for her every summer, like you said. He's no make-believe hero now.

DUNC: C'mon over here where it's shady. I won't bite.

             JOANIE moves next to him, takes another drink.

JOANIE: Even if you had come around, I wouldn't have let you in.

DUNC: You'd have let me in.

JOANIE: Unh-uh. I promised Carol-Ann.

DUNC: What? That you wouldn't see me?

JOANIE: Swore it on my mother's grave. If she's got one.

DUNC: Boy oh boy. And you stand there, doin' what? Workin' me over.

JOANIE: Who's working you over? Not me.

DUNC: Not much!

JOANIE: All you had to do was come around! So I could tell you not to come around!

Suddenly, JOANIE laughs. DUNC joins her.

We had some good times, huh?

DUNC: You bet we did.

JOANIE: Yeah. We did.

DUNC: Even if I do step around a bit—on principle. You're still my best girl. You know that.

JOANIE: Do I.

DUNC: Whole town knows it.

JOANIE: I wonder.

DUNC: Listen here, Joanie—what do you say. Next summer like clockwork, all right?

JOANIE: Shush, you.

DUNC: Kinda answer is that?

JOANIE shakes her head. He tries to kiss her. She backs away.

Maybe you've found yourself another summertime man.

JOANIE: Maybe I don't need one, now I'm a Valued Citizen.

DUNC: You are?

JOANIE: According to the mayor I am.

She draws a letter from her purse and hands it to him.

Here's the letter he says it in. Proof! They're printing that letter alongside my essay. Word for word. With pictures. And you'll be hearing me on the radio. If you happen to catch it.

DUNC: *(Handing back the letter.)* That's real nice, Joanie. Carol-Ann's gonna be proud of you.

JOANIE: Maybe. Anyways, she'll be surprised. I hate writing anything, she knows that—even a letter, even a grocery list. But I saw that contest advertised and I just said out loud to myself everything I felt—which I'm good at!—and then I wrote it all down, quick. And I won. *(Pause.)* You're looking good, Dunc Carr, you know that? You've kept your body real good.

DUNC: I've stayed slim, anyhow.

JOANIE. Slim and hard. Not like me. I've got whole sections of my body now, looking like the surface of the moon. Craters that deep!

DUNC: You still got the best legs in town.

JOANIE: That's not saying much.

DUNC: You know it, too. *(Moving in.)* Don't you?

JOANIE: Maybe.

DUNC: Maybe!

He starts to caress her.

JOANIE: Maybe that's one thing I've still got.

He kisses her. She tries to break away but he pulls her back. The scene heats up.

DUNC: Come on, Joanie.

JOANIE: No. I don't dare.

DUNC: My truck's right here.

He kisses her again, then leads her off.

Scene Two

The train station, moments later. CAROL-ANN stands up centre. There's a suitcase beside her. She sighs, picks up the suitcase and begins to move down centre. Suddenly JOANIE enters, on the run.

JOANIE: Carol-Ann!

CAROL-ANN: Mum! What's the matter?

JOANIE: Nothing. I'm just so glad to have you back. You look so good, so…I think you've grown. Have you grown? You look just—beautiful!

JOANIE hugs CAROL-ANN as DUNC enters, carrying JOANIE's paper bag.

DUNC: You, uh…you dropped this.

A very awkward moment.

My mother's gettin' off, too—supposed to be. Maybe you seen her.

CAROL-ANN: *(Very chilly.)* Yes.

DUNC: Good.

He begins to move down off; he hesitates.

Uh—you folks want a ride?

JOANIE: No! Thanks.

DUNC: I could easy drop you but, uh…well.

               He exits. Short silence. JOANIE tries to give CAROL-
               ANN a kiss on the cheek, but CAROL-ANN turns
               away.

JOANIE: You've cut your hair.

CAROL-ANN: You don't like it.

JOANIE: I like it, looks real pretty, only what's your Grandpa
               going to say? He's been cutting your hair since you
               were two years old.

CAROL-ANN: I knew you'd be mad.

JOANIE: I'm not mad, Carol-Ann. Look—I brought you a
               present. Open it, quick.

               CAROL-ANN refuses to accept the bag. JOANIE
               opens it and draws out the woolens.

               Hand-knit mitts and a scarf to match! Aren't they
               pretty? I looked at blue—the blue would've matched
               your eyes perfect. But somehow or other…

CAROL-ANN: Mitts. In this heat.

               JOANIE shoves the woolens back in the bag. CAROL-
               ANN starts to move off.

JOANIE: Aren't you going to wait for me? Carol-Ann, you wait
               for me!

               CAROL-ANN stops, sets down the suitcase but
               doesn't turn around.

               I want you to understand.

CAROL-ANN: I understand.

JOANIE: No! It's not like it looks. This whole summer, that's
               the first I've seen of him. It is! It just happened we
               were meeting the same train. We got talking—

CAROL-ANN: Stop it.

JOANIE: There'll be no dirty talk, is what I'm saying.

CAROL-ANN: It doesn't matter.

JOANIE: It mattered last summer.

CAROL-ANN: Well, it doesn't matter now.

JOANIE: Well! Then maybe you'll let me have that kiss. I really missed my little girl.

> *CAROL-ANN submits to a kiss.*

Now then—tell me about your trip. Was it fun?

CAROL-ANN: Can't you wait? It's awful hot out here.

JOANIE: And how's your Dad?

CAROL-ANN: Fine.

JOANIE: That's all? Just—fine?

CAROL-ANN: Can we go now?

JOANIE: There, you see? It does matter. You say it doesn't, but it does.

CAROL-ANN: Why him, that's all. Why someone who doesn't give a damn about you?

JOANIE: He gives a damn.

CAROL-ANN: All he is is a sleazy old drunk. Ask anyone! Do you know what they say about him behind his back? Know what they say about you?

> *JOANIE slaps CAROL-ANN. This shocks them both. CAROL-ANN begins to cry.*

JOANIE: I told you, Carol-Ann. This whole summer, that's the first I've—

CAROL-ANN: He doesn't care about you! He's got half a dozen women on the line, don't you know that? All he cares about is himself, and his stupid old witch of a mother, and his stupid buddies—

JOANIE: Aw, Carol-Ann...

CAROL-ANN: You promised! You broke your promise.

JOANIE: I did. I know I did. I'm sorry.

CAROL-ANN: I told you not to meet me. Didn't I tell you not to come and meet me? If you'd just stayed home!

JOANIE: I wore a dress, anyways, didn't I? At least I followed one order.

CAROL-ANN: Oh, Mum...

JOANIE: Sshh! Never mind.

She takes CAROL-ANN in her arms.

I'm just so glad to have you home, you'll never know how glad. And you know what? I've been giving things a lot of thought and—listen. I'd like you to do me a favour. I'd like you to try real hard, now you're home, to not be thinking about Toronto and Rose Coulee and comparing the two—

CAROL-ANN: *(Pulling away.)* OK, Mum.

JOANIE: Either in your mind or out loud, because they really aren't the same, you know? Sometimes places look— the place you come from can look a little shabby, sometimes, when you first come back.

CAROL-ANN: How would you know?

JOANIE: You can't be stealing the spotlight on Awards Night, like you used to, if your mind's way off in Toronto. Can you?

CAROL-ANN: No.

JOANIE: So you'll do that for me?

CAROL-ANN: Can we go now?

JOANIE: First, promise.

CAROL-ANN: Now?

JOANIE: It only takes a second to say, "I promise."

CAROL-ANN: I can't.

JOANIE: Why not? Something's happened, I can feel it. What's happened!

CAROL-ANN: I wasn't going to tell you yet.

                 She takes a deep breath.

                 I'm going back. I'm going to live with my Dad. He wants me to.

JOANIE: *(Very shaken.)* Well, sure he does. In a couple of years, when you're through school.

CAROL-ANN: Now. In a few weeks. I wasn't going to tell you right away, but—

JOANIE: You're not going.

CAROL-ANN: You always have to start in with all that—business!

JOANIE: You're not going!

CAROL-ANN: I am.

JOANIE: No. You're not. It's too soon.

CAROL-ANN: For what?

JOANIE: For me! I want you here.

CAROL-ANN: There's nothing here.

JOANIE: I'm here! And your Grandpa, and all your friends. People who care about you—

CAROL-ANN: Dad cares about me!

JOANIE: *(Beat.)* I know he does, Carol-Ann. But you can't go yet. You've got to stay till you're through school, I told you that before.

CAROL-ANN: I can't.

JOANIE: If you're doing this because of Dunc Carr—

CAROL-ANN: No, Mum.

JOANIE: *(Turning away.)* I can't spend another minute in this dress!

CAROL-ANN: I'm going to live with my Dad. You can't stop me if I want to go. I'm 16 now—old enough to choose. He's already got me enrolled in a school there, it's—

JOANIE: Not one more word!

CAROL-ANN: I'm going. I only came back to pack.

> *CAROL-ANN picks up the suitcase and exits. JOANIE stares after her. After a moment, she notices the paper bag, opens it again and draws out the scarf.*

JOANIE: She's right. A dumb present, in this heat. Even the blue would've been wrong.

> *She shoves the scarf back in the bag and exits slowly, as lights fade on the station. At blackout, JOANIE's voice is heard, recorded, reading her essay.*

VOICE-OVER: "Why I love Rose Coulee by Joanie Birrell.

"I love Rose Coulee because no matter where you live or how much money you've got, you can see the sky and smell the rain when it comes.

"I like being able to pick up the phone and call someone and talk ten minutes for no reason at all. And if you happen to get a wrong number, you can still talk ten minutes. Try that in the city sometime!

"I like knowing I can walk across town and say "Hi" to everyone, and greet dogs and babies by name and teenagers I've known since they were just a secret hope in their mother's heart (or a secret ambition in their father's!)

"I like just about everybody in this town, and the older they get the more I seem to like them. Especially the ladies. I like the old old ladies who call you

"Dearie" and slip their cool silky hand in yours, and ask you all about your life, and never complain about theirs but only laugh it off and walk away, and leave you staring at your empty hand, that never felt so full.

"I like …"

The recording is shut off.

Scene Three

> *JOANIE's house; the kitchen. Friday, supper-time. JOANIE and CAROL-ANN are at the table.*

JOANIE: Come on now, Carol-Ann. Eat up.

CAROL-ANN: I'm not hungry.

JOANIE: Eat up anyways.

CAROL-ANN: I hate stew. I hate everything on this plate.

JOANIE: Listen to you. You should be glad to have such a meal set in front of you. Look at all the things on that plate, that were once living but gave up their lives so you could have a nice wholesome—

> *CAROL-ANN shoves her plate aside.*

It was a joke, Carol-Ann.

> *She reaches out to brush CAROL-ANN's hair out of her face.*

I haven't seen you smile once since you got home. Did you know that? Haven't heard a word about your trip, either. Or your Dad. I notice you phoned him, though, last night. Talked 17 minutes—

CAROL-ANN: Collect.

JOANIE: More than you've talked to me all day. He's doing OK, then. Is he?

CAROL-ANN: Why?

JOANIE: I'm interested, why shouldn't I be? It's only natural. He must be interested in me, too, a little. He must sometimes ask about me.

               CAROL-ANN shrugs.

               See! What sort of things does he ask? I hope you don't make me sound too awful. I hope you don't tell him everything.

CAROL-ANN: What do you mean?

JOANIE: Like, you know, that I'm into a size 12.

CAROL-ANN: He doesn't give a damn what size you wear.

JOANIE: I'm only telling you one more time—eat up!

CAROL-ANN: I don't see why we have to have stew every single Friday night. In Toronto—

JOANIE: Eat!

               CAROL-ANN plays with her food.

               Stew's two-thirty-nine a pound, Carol-Ann.

CAROL-ANN: Aren't you ever going to learn metric? The whole world knows metric!

JOANIE: If you think that's true, you should spend a day with me behind the counter at Macleods. Hardly any of our customers have bothered to figure it out.

CAROL-ANN: Dad knows metric. So does Francesca.

JOANIE: Francesca?

CAROL-ANN: His girlfriend.

               JOANIE takes this like a fist in the stomach.

               What's the matter?

JOANIE: Francesca. Whoever heard of a name like that.

               She gets herself in hand.

What's she like, I wonder, this—Francesca. Do you mind telling me?

CAROL-ANN: She's not like Dunc Carr, that's for sure.

JOANIE: I bet she's pretty. Is she?

CAROL-ANN: I suppose.

JOANIE: Blonde?

CAROL-ANN: Auburn.

JOANIE: Long? Or short?

CAROL-ANN: Long. What else do you want to know? Curly or straight? Curly! Natural or permed? Natural.

JOANIE: I'm getting real tired of this, Carol-Ann. Every summer it's worse. You step down off that train and prance around here like everything in the place smelled like bad meat. Me especially!

CAROL-ANN: I don't see why you want to know what she's like. You're just going to hate her, anyway.

JOANIE: Maybe I want to know what I'm hating!

A silence.

You're right, Carol-Ann. You're completely right.

CAROL-ANN: I'll tell you what she's like. She's got a closet a mile long full of clothes, that's one thing. I mean, a mile. And she never goes anywhere, not even to the Safeway, without perfume. *(Hamming it up.)* She wouldn't even walk the dog without perfume, without perfume she feels absolutely naked!

JOANIE: Oh.

CAROL-ANN: Yeah.

JOANIE: I bet she's skinny, too.

CAROL-ANN: She looks like a model. She was a model, once, but now when they call her up she almost always turns them down. She's a fibre artist now. She's all right.

JOANIE: Where does she live, I wonder?

The silence says it.

Oh.

CAROL-ANN: Since April. I doubt if he'll marry her, though. Mum?

JOANIE: Why should he? He's already got her, doesn't he. Now he wants you.

The phone rings.

CAROL-ANN: He does.

JOANIE: *(Rising.)* He's going to be disappointed.

She picks up the phone.

Hello. Oh, yes! Well, thanks—thank you! I don't really see what's so good about it, but... Did you? Well, that's—well! I'm glad to hear that. I will, and thanks for calling!

She hangs up.

Phil Murray, Senior. Just wanted to say how much he enjoyed my essay in *The News*! *(She sits at the table.)* And what about you, Carol-Ann? Did you enjoy it?

CAROL-ANN: Well, sure, yeah, it was good...

JOANIE: Only?

CAROL-ANN: Only I naturally don't agree with it.

JOANIE: What part? What part don't you agree with?

CAROL-ANN: Well, I don't agree with any of it. But, I mean, it's still good.

JOANIE: Not even the part about the Men's and Boys' Store? You don't agree with that? Or where I talk about the old old ladies—

CAROL-ANN: I said it's good, didn't I? Just because I don't agree with it doesn't mean it isn't any good, does it?

JOANIE: I don't know.

CAROL-ANN: It doesn't.

JOANIE: Well, Mr. Murray liked it, anyways. He's already bought up six copies to send to all his relatives at the Coast!

CAROL-ANN: I'm glad you won, Mum. Honest. The pictures were nice.

JOANIE: I bet if your Dad had written that essay, you'd have liked it well enough.

CAROL-ANN: But he wouldn't have. He'd never have written any of those things.

JOANIE: He's not from here, that's why. He only moved here when he was 17, he's never really been considered—

CAROL-ANN: He likes Toronto! Where things happen.

JOANIE rises abruptly and exits, with the plates. She returns immediately and sits.

JOANIE: Listen, Carol-Ann. I was upstairs this afternoon—wandering around—and it suddenly hit me what we ought to do. We ought to knock out a wall! If we knocked out one wall, we could turn half the upstairs into one huge bedroom, all for you. Windows all around. And the other thing I decided was, it's time you had your own phone. If we're real careful, and count our pennies—

CAROL-ANN turns abruptly away.

A year ago you were begging for your own phone.

CAROL-ANN: I won't be here.

JOANIE: You'll be here.

CAROL-ANN: I won't.

JOANIE: You will. I can't let go of you, Carol-Ann, not yet. I'd
               like to be able to in a way, but—

               The phone begins to ring.

               I just can't. I'm going to hang onto you with my
               fingernails and teeth and toenails, if I have to.

CAROL-ANN: Like you did with Dad.

JOANIE: That was different.

CAROL-ANN: And look where that got you.

JOANIE: Answer it, for heaven's sake! Take a message.

               CAROL-ANN answers the phone.

CAROL-ANN: Hello? No, this is Carol-Ann. Not right now. OK, I'll
               tell her.

               She hangs up.

               Mrs. Sawchuck. *(Mimics.)* That essay just says it all!

               CAROL-ANN moves towards the door.

JOANIE: Where are you going? Carol-Ann. Come back here
               and sit down!

CAROL-ANN: Why?

JOANIE: I haven't excused you yet!

               CAROL-ANN slouches back to the table and sits.

               I could stand a round of crib, later on. You?

CAROL-ANN: I don't think so.

JOANIE: Maybe what you'd like is a nice hot bath. I've got
               some brand-new bath oil up there that Beryl gave me.
               Smells like a garden everything came up in! You
               know Beryl. I'd be glad to fill the tub for you

CAROL-ANN: I don't want a bath, OK?

JOANIE: I tell you what, Carol-Ann. From now on, I'm going to let you go to Toronto twice a year, instead of just once.

CAROL-ANN: I am going—to live with—my Dad.

JOANIE: You're not.

CAROL-ANN: If I was you, and you were me, you know what I'd do? I'd say, "Go!"

JOANIE: Oh no, you wouldn't.

CAROL-ANN: I'd know it was in your own best interests.

JOANIE: Don't talk to me about your best interests! Your best interests have been my first concern since you were two inches long!

CAROL-ANN: If that was true, you'd have made Dad happy.

JOANIE: That's an awful thing to say.

CAROL-ANN: You'd have given up that damn job at Macleods! You shouldn't have taken that job in the first place. Dad had a perfectly good job—

JOANIE: With the highways, part-time! And nowhere near enough money coming in. What good was it, talking about seeing the world—

CAROL-ANN: That's not the reason.

JOANIE: What?

CAROL-ANN: I've heard that story a hundred times. Maybe you've told it so often you even believe it. It's twisted, you've got it all twisted up. I know the reason you hung onto that job.

JOANIE: What's the reason then, Miss Smarty-Pants?

CAROL-ANN: It was fear. You were scared to death if he ever got out into the big wide world, you'd lose him. What a joke on you!

JOANIE: Stop it, Carol-Ann.

CAROL-ANN: All you had to do was give up that job—

JOANIE: I did give it up!

CAROL-ANN: That's not true.

JOANIE: I gave it up, and he left without me. He left without
               us, Carol-Ann.

               CAROL-ANN moves abruptly toward the door.

               Where are you going? Don't you go running to your
               Grandpa with this, do you hear me? He's sick enough
               as it is!

CAROL-ANN: He'll have to find out sooner or later. I'm all packed.

               *CAROL-ANN exits, slamming the door. JOANIE sits
               for a moment.*

JOANIE: What good was it—talking about seeing the world!
               And one day, Mr. Walker at the Macleods store, he
               said to me, "Joanie, you ever need to make a dollar,
               you come see me." So I did, and he gave me a job.

               She turns toward the door.

               The hardest part was not seeing you eight hours a
               day. Your Grandpa had to keep you, at the Clip'n
               Curl. You were underfoot, I guess, but no one ever
               complained—you were so cute, you were the cutest
               little thing.

               She turns back.

               And then one night…oh, things weren't going too
               good between me and your Dad, and one night he
               said if I didn't quit my job, he'd leave me—just like
               that. So the very next morning I told Mr. Walker I had
               to quit. And that night when I told your Dad he said,
               "Good." Only, about an hour later he said, "I think I'll
               just slip over to the Drake for a beer," and he did, and
               he didn't come back. I was just lucky Mr. Walker let

me have my job back. But I did quit—I did!

JOANIE exits.

Scene Four

The porch, Sunday morning. BERYL calls across the steps.

BERYL: So he says to me: Listen here, Beryl, I know you never liked me, always wondered why. And I says, well Dunc Carr, I'll tell you. You're a sycophant.

BERYL explodes with laughter.

The look on his face! Doesn't have a clue what it means, right? And all his buddies—all his Plains Inn buddies—standing there, looking on. So finally one of them says, what's that mean, Dunc? What's a sycophant, anyways? And he says—listen, you know what he says? Joanie?

JOANIE at the screened door, wearing a dressing gown.

Says, hell, it's obvious, ain't it. Means I'm a goddamn hunk. No kidding! That's Dunc for you. More guts than a slaughterhouse. What's the matter? This is your favourite subject I'm talking about.

JOANIE: It's never been that.

BERYL: *(Meaning high on the list.)* It's been up there.

JOANIE: She's not talking to me now. At all. I feel like I'm living in an empty house…

BERYL: Come out here, Joanie. Come on.

JOANIE steps out onto the porch.

JOANIE: I should've seen it coming, Beryl. Why didn't I? If I'd just used my head! I shouldn't have let her go off to Toronto the first time, let alone twice more. I don't know why I did.

BERYL: Never mind that. Can't do a thing about it now.

JOANIE: I never thought he'd want her full-time. Not yet. I've tried everything I can think of to stop her. Threats. Pleading. Bribery. I keep telling her she can't go...

BERYL: And?

JOANIE: She just keeps packing!

                The phone starts ringing.

                And that damn phone, it hasn't stopped ringing.

BERYL: Well, what do you expect? You're a celebrity now. The genuine article. Pretty soon we'll all be saying We Knew Her When. Aren't you going to answer it? Joanie?

JOANIE: What?

                The phone stops ringing.

BERYL: Never mind.

JOANIE: I keep getting these—awful pictures in my head...can't sleep at all and when I do I keep having dreams... My mother! I keep seeing my mother and she never speaks, you know, she never says a word or smiles. Just stands there—big frown, cold—and before I know it turns and goes. That's all—just goes. You'd think she'd say something, wouldn't you, Beryl?

BERYL: You'd better sit down, Joanie. I mean it.

JOANIE: And also, of all things. I've been dreaming about those baby clothes—you remember all those clothes I knit for Carol-Ann, before she was born, how I kept making 'em and throwing 'em out, making 'em and throwing 'em out, it nearly drove Boone crazy.

BERYL: I'm only saying it one more time. Sit, or I'll sit on you!

                JOANIE seems to notice BERYL for the first time.

JOANIE: What are you doing here so early?

BERYL: Couldn't sleep. Tossed and turned all night long. Well, I rolled around a bit. Good for me. Exercise. Not the kind of bedtime exercise I prefer, and require, and deserve—God, how I deserve it. But anyway.

JOANIE: *(Sitting.)* Oh, Beryl…

BERYL: You sounded awful on the phone last night. If I could have, I'd have come right over.

JOANIE: Were they mad I called?

BERYL: What if they were. Where are they going to find another cocktail hostess who can draw men to the place like flies, huh? Besides, it was a slow night.

JOANIE: I had to talk to someone.

                   CAROL-ANN appears at the screen door.

BERYL: Well! Here she is now. Miss Toronto.

CAROL-ANN: *(Entering.)* Hello, Beryl.

BERYL: Welcome home.

CAROL-ANN: I see you've painted your house.

BERYL: What do you think? Like it?

CAROL-ANN: If you want to know what I think—

JOANIE: She noticed it right away. Didn't you, Carol-Ann?

CAROL-ANN: I couldn't help it.

JOANIE: Fetch us a coffee, Carol-Ann. And some of that chocolate cake I made.

CAROL-ANN: At nine in the morning?

                   JOANIE and BERYL both turn to glare at CAROL-ANN. CAROL-ANN exits.

BERYL: Doesn't like it, huh.

JOANIE: Sure she does.

                BERYL gives her a look.

                Well, what if she doesn't? You like it, and if you like it,
                Beryl, I like it.

                The phone rings, just once.

BERYL: It's a real smart shade of purple.

JOANIE: It stands out, all right.

CAROL-ANN: *(At the screen door.)* It's for you.

JOANIE: Say I'm out. Well, I am out!

                CAROL-ANN disappears again.

                To top it off, he's got a girlfriend now. Live-in.
                Francesca—that's her name. Seems to me a person
                with a name like that ought to be enough for one man,
                but no! Francesca. Spends half her life spraying
                herself with perfume. Skinny as a rake, too.

BERYL: Well, that's a stroke of luck. She won't last. Those
                skinny ones don't. Some little calamity comes along,
                they drop twenty pounds and blow away, like bits of
                paper in the wind. They do. I read that somewhere.
                Or if I didn't, I should have.

                *CAROL-ANN enters with a tray, which she sets
                down.*

                Thanks, honey. I see you got your hair cut.

CAROL-ANN: Yes. Like it?

BERYL: I like it. Wonder if your Grandpa did?

JOANIE: Beryl.

BERYL: Did he?

CAROL-ANN: Who knows? He pretended he didn't see it. That's
                what people do around here. You can stick

something right under their noses and they'll stare right through it, if they want to.

BERYL: *(To JOANIE.)* Don't think she's in any danger of settling back in.

CAROL-ANN: You're right about that.

BERYL: *(To CAROL-ANN.)* Guess you know who you're hurting, huh.

JOANIE: Never mind, Beryl.

BERYL: Do you?

CAROL-ANN: I'm not doing it to hurt her.

BERYL: Then why?

CAROL-ANN: To help myself.

BERYL: You've got a lifetime for that.

CAROL-ANN: I don't want to fight with you, Beryl.

CAROL-ANN begins to move off.

JOANIE: Where are you going?

BERYL: Makes you look like an angel—that haircut.

JOANIE: Carol-Ann, I asked you a question!

CAROL-ANN: For a walk.

JOANIE: Where to? Not that gloomy old graveyard.

CAROL-ANN: I like the graveyard. *(Exits.)*

JOANIE: If I told her to go there, it's the last place you'd find her!

BERYL: Bet you're glad I came, huh. I bet you can't believe the influence I have on that child. Aw, don't worry, kid. You'll stop her.

JOANIE: I couldn't stop Boone, could I?

BERYL: This is a little different.

JOANIE: Is it?

BERYL: Sure it is. You've got rights. In fact, know what you should do? You should call a lawyer.

JOANIE: A lawyer! Who's going to pay for that.

BERYL: Maybe your father...

JOANIE: With what, his life savings?

BERYL: Then go to the bank.

JOANIE: Even if I did, and fought him and won, what would I have at the end? A daughter who hates me, and blames me all her life. She would, I know it. She's just like him, Beryl, she's just exactly like him, she's even...she's got the exact same look in her eye, like she's already shut the door on me and left. How do you fight that, I'd like to know. What lawyer can fight that?

BERYL: Well then, maybe you should help her pack. Don't look at me like that. She'd be going anyway, in a few years.

JOANIE: I can't believe I'm hearing this.

BERYL: Sometimes it's better, if they want to go, to just say— go.

JOANIE: Being a mother, you'd know this.

BERYL: OK, I'm not a mother.

JOANIE: That's right!

BERYL: But sometimes I think maybe you—

JOANIE: Beryl, just drop it! I'm not real anxious to be told all the things I've done wrong in my life. I already know them by heart.

BERYL: I wish you could hear yourself. You won't fight and you won't give in—

JOANIE: Maybe on the outside it looks simple. Maybe to you. Maybe it looks like I ought to—give in gracefully. But Beryl, you know, I don't—

BERYL: Joanie—

JOANIE: —know how! *(Beginning to cry.)* Never did. Can't!

BERYL: I know, kid. Never mind. Here, come and sit.

            JOANIE sits next to BERYL, who throws an arm across her shoulders.

            Don't pay any attention to me. Hardly anyone ever hung around me long enough to turn into a problem. Or maybe I was the problem—but what a problem, huh! Maybe I was their problem and they solved it. And, anyway, I let them. So who am I to talk? *(Big sigh.)* I guess under the circumstances there's only one thing to do.

            They look at one another, then at the cake. They whoop and lunge for it.

            See, this is the way I look at it. No matter how bad things get, there's always chocolate cake. Chocolate brownies. Chocolate chip cookies. And men. In that order. Hopefully.

            A silence

            There's those cats again, peeing in your sandbox. You should get rid of that sandbox.

JOANIE: I know.

BERYL: You turned everything he ever touched into something sacred.

JOANIE: I did not, Beryl.

BERYL: Ha!

JOANIE: OK—it goes.

BERYL: When?

JOANIE: First thing this fall.

BERYL: Yeah. *(With a sigh.)* Well, I guess I can go home now. I guess now that I've made you as miserable as you can possibly be, I can go home.

                BERYL rises.

JOANIE: No, Beryl, I feel better. Calmer. If I can stay calm, maybe I can think of what to do.

BERYL: Meanwhile, I'll get this gorgeous body back where it belongs. In bed. Unless you want to tell me what happened at the station Thursday.

JOANIE: I already told you.

BERYL: You roughed it in. It's the details I'm waiting for. I'm waiting to be forced to sit through all the sordid details.

JOANIE: What happened shouldn't have, that's clear.

BERYL: *(Pause.)* At the bar last night, they were all talking about you. Were your ears burning?

JOANIE: Who was?

BERYL: All the boys.

JOANIE: They were?

BERYL: They sure were. They were all talking about your essay.

JOANIE: *(Pleased.)* Oh!

BERYL: *(Laughs.)* She fell for it.

                She begins to move off.

                That essay's the last thing they think of when they think of you. Believe me, I know.

                BERYL exits. JOANIE exits.

VOICE-OVER: "I like the way people are good to one another. Like when a certain person kept telling that same joke about the plugged-up bull every single morning right up until the morning he died, nobody ever let on. And if another certain person got fed up being stuck in a wheelchair and started to run around town on her ride-em lawn mower, and scatter scraps for the birds, nobody minds. Instead what they do is, they start saving up scraps to give her.

"I like the names of places here—the Dew Drop Inn and the Clip'n Curl, and I like the smell of tobacco and wool that hits you when you open the door of the Men's and Boy's Store. And I think it's a shame the way businesses are fighting to stay alive. People should remember the dollars they spend at home come back to them but the dollars they spend away..."

The recording is shut off.

Scene Five

The kitchen, about a week later. There's music playing—"When a Man Loves a Woman," sung by Percy Sledge. JOANIE, still in the dressing gown, moves to the record player and turns up the volume. CAROL-ANN is at the table, reading. JOANIE sways to the music for a moment, then turns to CAROL-ANN.

JOANIE: Dance with me, Carol-Ann. Come on. Didn't I teach you everything you know?

CAROL-ANN: You're not dressed. You hardly ever get dressed any more.

JOANIE: I get dressed for work.

CAROL-ANN: Half the time you don't even brush your hair.

JOANIE: Please?

CAROL-ANN rises reluctantly and dances with her mother.

CAROL-ANN: All these old records. Next you'll be playing Cohen.

JOANIE: Sshhh. *(They dance quietly for a moment.)* Isn't this better? Isn't it better when we're nice to each other?

CAROL-ANN: I guess when it comes down to it, I'm not a very nice person any more.

JOANIE: I think maybe you'll improve with age.

CAROL-ANN: I'm not like this in Toronto. I'm not! *(Timidly.)* You can't catch the wind in a bottle, don't you know that? If you do, all you end up with is air.

JOANIE: Oh, that's real pretty. I know exactly who you got that from.

CAROL-ANN: *(Pulling away.)* See what I mean? It's hopeless.

CAROL-ANN turns the record player off.

JOANIE: I spent my whole life aching for the mother I never had, and you want to walk away from yours.

CAROL-ANN: It's not my fault this is happening. It's not! You shouldn't have hung around here after Dad left. I don't know why you did.

JOANIE: Where was I supposed to go?

CAROL-ANN: Anywhere!

JOANIE: Anywhere. With two mouths to feed.

CAROL-ANN: I'd have cleared out, that's for sure. I'd never let myself get stuck in a place with—purple houses, and people who look right through them.

JOANIE: Oh! Now it's Beryl's house.

CAROL-ANN: That house! The whole town knows how bad it looks but to her face what do they say? That's real nice, Beryl, that really stands out.

JOANIE: You don't think people should be kind?

CAROL-ANN: I bet there isn't a purple house in the whole of Toronto!

JOANIE: Well, that's one thing we've got that they haven't!

CAROL-ANN: Dad travelled all over the world after he left here. He was restless, that's why. And I'm the same—I take after him. I used to think there was something wrong with me, walking around here with a hole inside me bigger than an ocean...

        JOANIE takes CAROL-ANN's hand.

JOANIE: Is that what you do in that gloomy old graveyard? Dream about your Dad? It's a funny place to go for that.

CAROL-ANN: *(Pulling her hand away.)* At least in the graveyard, people aren't always saying this is the place to be!

        A train whistle sounds, off in the distance.

JOANIE: Listen! When I was little—I probably told you this. Whenever I heard a train whistle, know what I thought it meant?

CAROL-ANN: Someone had died.

JOANIE: I thought some soul had just slipped free of a body and gone soaring up to heaven, and the train was singing that soul goodbye! I did. Now a train whistle is one sound I can hardly stand to hear.

CAROL-ANN: Now comes heaven.

JOANIE: When I was little...I couldn't wait to die. 'Cause I knew there was a heaven and I liked the way it looked. I knew when I got there I'd run right up to Jesus where he'd be sitting in his long white dress surrounded by all those kids. And if I looked past him, I'd see lambs and lions playing together by some stream and a whole field full of wild flowers and a sky that was always perfectly blue except for a rainbow off in the distance, blinking off and on like the neon sign on the Dew Drop Inn!

CAROL-ANN: Leave it, Mum.

JOANIE: You have different ideas, when you're little. All those ideas of mine, they didn't last too long. Went walking out the door one day when I was five—

CAROL-ANN: Listen to me! You're wasting your time, do you understand? It won't do any good! You can sluff around here all you like in that dirty old dressing gown, and talk about all that stuff, but I'm still going. I'm going! There's two kinds of people in the world. Some leave, and some get left. And I know what I'm not going to be!

JOANIE: Carol-Ann—

CAROL-ANN runs to the screen door and exits. JOANIE stares after her, frozen. The light fades gradually to a single spot, trained on the phone. Meanwhile, the recording is heard:

VOICE-OVER: "I like knowing in advance how a day's going to shape up. Who you'll probably see and where and how they'll look. And if they've got a new dress or something, knowing it's new and being able to say how nice it is.

                 "I guess, when it comes down to it, I like Rose Coulee because it's where I come from. And when I'm too old to know where I am anymore, all I'll have to do is glance up at the P&H Elevator at the south end of Main Street and it'll still have Rose Coulee written across the top. That's if I can still see that far!"

                 End of voice-over. JOANIE is on the phone.

JOANIE: Hello...Francesca? This is Joanie calling, this is Carol-Ann's Mum? I need to talk to Boone. Oh...no! No, I can't, I really can't, I've got to talk to him now, tonight! Isn't there any way...? I see. I guess I better do that, I guess I have to. See, the thing is, what I phoned to say is there's no point expecting Carol-Ann because she's not coming, she's not—coming, she's going to stay here with her Mum. Well sure, of her own free will, I can't lock her up, can I? She's had a change of heart, that's all. And the reason she hasn't told Boone is she's afraid to, afraid to hurt his feelings—thinks so much of her Dad! Now this part is real important. You've got to tell him if he really cares about his daughter, now's the time to show it. Tell him that exactly. Tell him he's to write her a letter, saying he's been thinking things over and he's decided she ought to stay here till she's through school. And he's not to mention this phone call at all, ever, period. Make sure you say that. Well, maybe so—I don't know about that, all I know is people can't always get their way, even Boone...even Boone can't always get his way. You can tell him that, too, if you want. I don't care what you tell him as long as he for once in his life does the one decent thing there is to do!

JOANIE slams down the receiver.

Scene Six

The porch, a week later. 9:30 p.m. CAROL-ANN sits on the steps, brushing her hair. She wears a nightgown. JOANIE enters, in a shapeless polyester uniform. She sits wearily.

JOANIE: Oh! Feels good just to sit.

CAROL-ANN: Busy tonight?

JOANIE: Busy! I don't know what it is about night shopping. Brings 'em all out. You're all dressed for bed. How come? You're not sick?

CAROL-ANN: I've been sitting here trying to remember something.

JOANIE: What?

CAROL-ANN: That song Dad used to sing me, when I was little. That one with the knight in it, and the beggar, and the bird...

JOANIE: Cohen. It would be Cohen—it was always Cohen! If it wasn't for me, you'd have ended up being called

Suzanne for sure. Or Marianne. Instead of Carol-Ann.
Which is much prettier! I bet he still likes Cohen.

CAROL-ANN: Guess again.

JOANIE: Go on, he must.

CAROL-ANN: He's progressed—you know?

JOANIE: Well, I haven't. I'm like that hot pink-and-lavender
wallpaper in Beryl's downstairs bathroom. I got
stuck back about 1969. (*Studying CAROL-ANN's face.*)
Are you missing your Dad, Carol-Ann? If you are,
you can phone him. I'll treat.

CAROL-ANN: It's all right.

JOANIE: It's kind of funny you haven't heard from him. How
long has it been?

CAROL-ANN: Only a few days. He called me.

JOANIE: What'd he have to say for himself?

CAROL-ANN: Not much.

JOANIE: Must've said something—

CAROL-ANN: Mum?

JOANIE: What, Carol-Ann.

CAROL-ANN: Want me to brush your hair?

JOANIE: Would you? I'd really like that.

> *CAROL-ANN kneels behind JOANIE and begins to
> brush.*

Oh—feels so good! Your Dad used to do that for me.
And, before that, I could sometimes get your
Grandpa to, if I talked real nice. 'Course, at that time
I had hair right down to my knees. It used to make
your Grandpa awful nervous, all that hair. He used to
sometimes catch me prancing past the Clip 'n Curl,
and he'd call me in and say—

CAROL-ANN: Tame that goddamn mane!

JOANIE: *(Laughs.)* That's your Grandpa.

CAROL-ANN: And then?

JOANIE: What are you doing, Carol-Ann, humouring me?

CAROL-ANN: Go on.

JOANIE: Well—and then. He'd threaten to sit me down right there and give me a brush-cut. A lot of good it did. The minute he turned his back, I was gone, I was down at the Dew Drop Inn, sitting in a booth with Beryl. She was real pretty in those days, you'd be surprised. The two of us, what a pair. We lived—practically lived—at the Dew Drop Inn. After supper, especially, you'd always find us there, waiting. For the farm boys! Sometimes it'd be way past dark before they'd finally roll in. First they'd line up at the front counter—pretending not to see us—a dozen of them, sometimes, and every one of them brown from the sun and strong and...hair still wet from the shower. By the time their hair was dry, they'd have managed by some coincidence to find their way to our booth! Those boys. You could smell the fresh air on them, you actually could, it was as sweet as perfume. I remember this one time, Old Mr. Kee, that ran the place—I don't know why I'm telling you this—one time as he was setting down my Coke he said to me, "Drink it down slow, Joanie," only he didn't mean the Coke—I saw that right away. I saw, if I wasn't careful, those nights at the Dew Drop Inn, with those boys—fresh air boys!—would one day, when I looked back on them, seem to have been washed away in a minute, like a drink you gulped down too fast. Old Mr. Kee. He was right, too. 'Cause just after that I met your Dad, and those times—those boys—were all behind me. I didn't regret it then, not at first, but I sure did—after. Sometimes, even now, I...

CAROL-ANN: What?

JOANIE: That's enough, Carol-Ann. Let me have the brush.

                  JOANIE begins to brush CAROL-ANN's hair.

CAROL-ANN: You've never told that part before.

JOANIE: I don't know why I did now. Maybe to make you think. Appreciate!

CAROL-ANN: Tell about when you first met my Dad.

JOANIE: You don't want to hear that again.

CAROL-ANN: Sure I do.

JOANIE: It's not much of a story, anyways.

CAROL-ANN: I like it. I like to try and picture it.

JOANIE: I think maybe I've told it once too often.

CAROL-ANN: Go on.

JOANIE: I had my eye on this boy—a boy called Jamie. And he definitely had his eye on me! He'd started picking me up on Sunday afternoons in his Dad's half-ton and taking me out to look at the crops. At least, that's what we told your Grandpa! It was just fun, just—innocent. It was really Jamie I was waiting for, this one night, at the Dew Drop Inn. But I looked up, all of a sudden, and there he was—your Dad—staring at me. I turned away, I remember, and then I turned back. Couldn't help it. And all the prance I know went out of my step, and the saucy look your Grandpa always grumbled about dropped right off my face. He made me different, your Dad.

CAROL-ANN: Better.

JOANIE: Or worse. Not as brave. *(Beat.)* I don't know why he picked me, I really don't. But I know why I picked him. He was burning up inside. You could feel the heat in him, like a fire just below the skin. *(Catches herself.)* He always had a book in his pocket, and almost before he said hello he'd want to give you some idea out of that book—

CAROL-ANN: He's still like that.

JOANIE: Like it was a gift, like another boy might give you flowers. He'd drive right by a whole lane full of free lilacs and never think to pick one, but he'd hand you an idea like it was something just as pretty. It was, too, usually. I thought so, anyways, but what did I know? My favourite subject at school was noon hour! Not like you, Carol-Ann.

CAROL-ANN: Are you sorry?

JOANIE: For what?

CAROL-ANN: For marrying him.

JOANIE: How could I be? I got you, didn't I?

                JOANIE hugs CAROL-ANN. CAROL-ANN rises and moves to the screen door.

                Carol-Ann? It was nice of you to brush my hair. Just like old times.

CAROL-ANN: Mum? Do you think you'll ever go to Toronto?

JOANIE: Don't start on that, Carol-Ann. I've been on my feet since ten this morning. Why would I?

CAROL-ANN: I don't know. For a visit.

JOANIE: Who would I visit?

CAROL-ANN: Just to see it, even.

JOANIE: Shut the door, Carol-Ann, we'll be slapping mosquitoes all night long.

CAROL-ANN: Aren't you curious?

JOANIE: I guess not. I guess I just wasn't born curious.

CAROL-ANN: I'll never understand that.

JOANIE: Why is it, I'd like to know, I've got a whole collection of faults, but somehow that one always ends up being the worst!

CAROL-ANN: *(After a moment.)* Goodnight, Mum.

JOANIE: 'Night, Carol-Ann.

> *CAROL-ANN exits. JOANIE leans back, closes her eyes. Deepening moonlight denotes the passage of time, about an hour. JOANIE has been asleep but wakes with a start. There's music playing very softly, off.*

Mumma? Who's out there? Is someone out there?

> *DUNC enters cautiously. JOANIE rises.*

I told you, never, never—

DUNC: I know.

JOANIE: This is the last place!

DUNC: I said I know.

JOANIE: What's wrong?

> *DUNC tries to answer, can't.*

Hang on a bit.

> *She opens the screen door, leans in, listens, calls softly.*

Carol-Ann?

> *She closes the door.*

It'll be all right, I guess. Till the music stops.

DUNC: Sure?

> *JOANIE sits, pats the step.*

JOANIE: Saved you my best chair.

> *DUNC sits next to her.*

What time is it, anyways?

DUNC: Eleven, almost.

JOANIE: I must've dropped off. Admiring the man in the moon.

DUNC: Well, now you can admire me instead.

JOANIE: I don't know why I'd want to do that, Dunc Carr.

DUNC: Aren't I better than some old shadow on the moon?

JOANIE: That old shadow keeps his distance.

> *DUNC seems about to rise to the challenge, then his face clouds. He looks away. JOANIE turns her face to the moon.*

There's more up there than shadows. Did you know that? There's footprints.

DUNC: Sure there is. Whose?

JOANIE: The astronauts'. They haven't gone away, and they're not going. Not for a thousand years. It's true. *(Abruptly.)* You look awful.

DUNC: They put my mother back in hospital.

JOANIE: Oh, no. When?

DUNC: Last night. She won't be gettin' out this time.

JOANIE: Sure she will.

DUNC: No. They said not.

JOANIE: What do they know.

> *In the distance, a train whistle sounds. Both turn towards the sound.*

DUNC: Eastbound.

> *He checks his watch.*

On time. They've got her hooked up to so many machines, she don't even look human. Looks more like an octopus. Looks like if she had to sneeze, she'd snap in two.

JOANIE: She'll be OK.

DUNC: Maybe.

JOANIE: She will.

DUNC: When my Dad went down…I saw him go. It was like somebody reached out and switched off a lamp. One minute he was there, then it turned dark. This is harder.

JOANIE: *(After a moment.)* My mother went a different way— very different! Did I ever tell you how? Walked out the front door one morning when I was five. Left the kettle boiling on the stove and on the kitchen table a half-finished paperback with the page she'd got to marked by a Kleenex and three—three—safety pins twisted all out of shape. Twisted up and tossed in the ashtray. Didn't take a thing with her—not even a comb. Now here's a question for you. Ever thought how nice it'd be if you could freeze time?

DUNC: Nobody can do that.

JOANIE: Somebody did—up there. That old moon's got footprints frozen right smack across its face. I like thinking about that. I like thinking about the very second that astronaut put his foot down on the moon, and how that second is frozen there. For a thousand years! What's the matter?

DUNC: You're a funny one. Well, what's the point? You can't see those footprints, anyways.

JOANIE: Doesn't matter. They're there. And that means somebody—one person—found a way to freeze a little bit of time. You wouldn't want all of it, that's for sure. A minute here and there. Maybe you wouldn't even want to freeze it, exactly—maybe just stretch it out a bit. Like, for instance, there's that minute—that split second—my mother tossed down that last safety pin. If I could've grabbed that minute, and stretched it out, something tells me she'd have never got away. *(Beat.)* Listen to me, doing all the talking…

DUNC: It's all right. I like to hear you talk.

JOANIE: You do? You never told me that.

DUNC: Can't do everything at one time, can I?

             He grins, glances away.

             I see Beryl's gone and painted her house.

JOANIE: She has.

DUNC: Stands out, don't it.

JOANIE: It does.

             They laugh. A train whistle sounds, far away.

             The music's stopped.

             Both listen, briefly.

DUNC: You think I better go?

JOANIE: I don't know. She ought to be asleep by now.

DUNC: Then how come you're so jittery? Maybe it's me, givin' you the jitters.

JOANIE: It's awful quiet all of a sudden. Isn't it?

DUNC: Maybe I ought to slide on over one of these nights, and get you over those jitters.

JOANIE: I don't see why it's all of sudden so quiet. I'm just going to slip upstairs and check on her.

             She rises and opens the door.

             Don't you run away, Dunc Carr, I'm not through with you yet.

             JOANIE exits. DUNC stands, lights a cigarette. Suddenly, a wail of anguish sounds from within.

DUNC: Joanie?

JOANIE throws open the screen door and runs down the steps, carrying a letter.

Joanie!

JOANIE: Take me to the station!

DUNC: What?

JOANIE: I should've known! I should've known! Take me to the station!

DUNC: What's wrong?

JOANIE: Never mind—I'll go myself! *(Starts off.)*

DUNC: All right, I'll take you. But the train's gone, Joanie. You heard it. She's already been 'n gone!

They exit.

End of Act One.

Act Two

Scene One

> *The porch, about six weeks later. A Sunday in early October. DUNC enters, wearing a jacket over his usual clothes. He climbs the steps, knocks on the screen door, waits, knocks again, very loud and insistent. JOANIE, in a dressing gown, appears at the door.*

JOANIE: Well, if it isn't.

DUNC: You alone?

JOANIE: No.

DUNC: I thought maybe you'd have run the gamut.

JOANIE: I managed to find one more.

DUNC: Good for you.

> *He sits.*

JOANIE: What do you think you're doing?

DUNC: Waitin'.

JOANIE: For what.

DUNC: To say what I come to say.

JOANIE: Honest to God, Dunc Carr, your timing's way off!

DUNC: Why? It's Sunday. Way past noon. A reasonable time for company.

JOANIE: I've got company.

DUNC: If I remember right, this house has two doors. Either you tell him which one to use, or I will.

JOANIE: You wouldn't dare.

DUNC gives her a look.

Never mind about him. Just talk. Make it snappy.

DUNC: You gonna come out here, or do I have to yell at you through the screen?

JOANIE: It's freezing out there.

DUNC: No, it's not, it's fine. Indian Summer.

JOANIE enters, sulkily.

Now sit down. Would you please sit?

JOANIE sits.

What I come to say is simple. This has got to stop.

JOANIE: What?

DUNC: Don't play dumb. You got the whole town talkin' about you—I guess you know that. I guess maybe you know and don't care. In six weeks only, you got yourself a reputation as bad as any I ever heard of.

JOANIE: I've had some fun.

DUNC: People looked the other way, at first. They felt bad for you, that's why, because of Carol-Ann. But now they're talkin'. Christ, it's a new story every morning.

JOANIE: Who I come home with—or don't—is no business of yours.

She rises abruptly, steps up onto the porch. He grabs her.

DUNC: Half of them are married, Joanie.

JOANIE: So?

DUNC: What's got into you? You surely don't plan on
            keepin' this up? Lettin' yourself get used?

JOANIE: You got it completely backwards. They're the ones
            getting used—by me!

            She pulls violently away from him.

            I spent my whole life, letting people tell me when
            they're coming and when they're going—mostly
            going! Not any more. I'm the one doing the telling
            now. I'm saying, "Hey you, take me home!" and in
            the morning I'm saying, "Now clear out." And you
            know what? They do it. And that's not all. It feels
            good! It feels so damn good, I'm starting to see why
            everyone's been doing it to me!

DUNC: You're not includin' me, I hope.

JOANIE: Why not?

DUNC: You better not be includin' me!

JOANIE: You checked in and out of here like you owned the
            place, two summers in a row.

DUNC: You didn't complain too loud. Seems to me that
            arrangement suited you fine!

JOANIE: But when Carol-Ann ran off—when I could have
            really used you—where were you? Nowhere to be
            found!

DUNC: I had a few problems, myself, remember? Nothin'
            major. A mother dyin' in hospital, is all. Lyin' in that
            goddamn hospital—

JOANIE: All right!

DUNC: I didn't see you beatin' a path across town to be with
            me. Not too often. Not even once! Maybe I could have
            used a little help—did you think of that? You didn't
            think of anyone but Joanie!

JOANIE: Maybe if you had a daughter that ran off and left
            you—

DUNC: She's alive, isn't she? At least she's alive! You can pick up the phone and call her, you can even see her if you want to, you could go down there and see her, and maybe bring her home. Why don't you? That's what everyone's sayin'. Why doesn't she just go and fetch Carol-Ann home, instead of throwin' herself at other women's men!

JOANIE: If you've come here to pick a fight—

DUNC: No. I haven't come for that. I thought maybe I could help you out.

JOANIE: I don't know why you'd want to do that, Dunc Carr. I might get to count on it. Then where would you be.

DUNC: Oh, for Chrissakes, Joanie—cut the crap. For once just cut the crap! Don't you think I know what goes on in your head?

JOANIE: You don't know!

DUNC: I know. The boys, they couldn't ever figure you out. There goes Joanie, what a waste. That's as far as they got. But I sat down and I figured you out, and I figured right 'cause you let me in. I'm talkin' about before, when nobody got in. You let me in! Why'd you do that, Joanie? Huh? Do you even know? Now look. I want you to settle down and behave yourself.

JOANIE: Why should I?

DUNC: 'Cause you're not doin' yourself any favours!

JOANIE: Know what I think? I think now your mother's gone, you've got your eye out for a new cook.

DUNC: I don't need a goddamn cook.

JOANIE: A housemaid, then. Someone to wash your smelly socks.

DUNC: I don't remember askin' you to move in. Did I ask you that?

JOANIE: Well, what is it, then? Scared I'm going to finish up with the boys at the Drake and start in on your buddies over at the Plains Inn? Well, guess what? I am!

DUNC moves as if to strike her, stops himself. JOANIE moves close to him.

Give me a kiss.

DUNC: Jesus!

JOANIE: Come on.

DUNC: I just about knocked you fiat. You just about made me.

JOANIE: Just a little one.

DUNC: Oh, no you don't. I'm not fallin' for that.

JOANIE: Come on.

DUNC: What brings this on?

JOANIE: Please!

DUNC: Joanie, you know...

He glances around, then kisses her quickly.

JOANIE: Is that the best you can do?

DUNC: There's a time and a place.

JOANIE: You didn't use to care about that.

DUNC: You didn't use to pass it around!

She begins to turn away. He grabs her, gives her a real kiss, draws away.

JOANIE: You're looking good, Dunc Carr.

DUNC: *(Pleased.)* Shit.

JOANIE: I mean it. How've you kept yourself so good?

DUNC: I don't know. Ridin'.

JOANIE:	Riding! You like horses, don't you? I'm glad. I like a man who's good to animals.

DUNC kisses her again, then starts to caress her. She responds briefly, then suddenly pulls back.

Now. Dunc Carr, get off my property.

DUNC:	What? You better be kiddin'! You're kickin' me off?
JOANIE:	You got it.
DUNC:	After what I done?
JOANIE:	What have you done!
DUNC:	Come over here, all set to help you out. I was even gonna forget all that talk I been hearin'—
JOANIE:	Clear out!
DUNC:	If I clear out of here now, I won't be back.
JOANIE:	That'll break my heart.

She opens the door. DUNC slams the door shut and pins her against the wall.

DUNC:	You don't talk to me like that! You hear me? You never talk like that to me! You! I don't know what's got into you but I'll tell you somethin'. I hardly recognize you. You know what you've turned into? Garbage. You're just a piece of rotten stinkin' garbage!
JOANIE:	If that's what I am, what are you? Buzzing around!
DUNC:	They warned me—I didn't believe it. I should've. If she's not garbage, where's her husband? That's what they said. Been sayin' it for years. How come people keep runnin' out on her, if she's not stinkin' garbage!

He sees this has hit home. A silence.

I don't know why I said that. That's a lie.

JOANIE opens the screen door.

Joanie? I thought we had somethin'—you and me.

JOANIE: I'll tell you what we had. A big fat nothin'.

JOANIE exits, closing the inside door. DUNC stares after her briefly, then strides off. Lights rise on the kitchen. JOANIE stands for a while with her back against the door. She moves across the kitchen and speaks to an invisible man—calmly at first, then in a screech.

Get out. Get out, get out, get out!

She grabs something and throws it.

Get out!

She covers her face with her hands. Lights fade on the porch and dim on the kitchen. The phone begins to ring. It seems to ring forever. Finally she answers it.

Hello. Who is this? I don't remember you. I still don't remember. What do you want?

She slams down the receiver. The phone rings again. She answers it on the second ring.

I tell you what. Maybe I'll consider it, on one condition. You've got to tell me who said to call. I'm curious, that's why, I like to know who's recommended me. I don't know anyone by that name. Well, I don't. Now, what I want you to do is listen real close. What's coming up is a message for him—whoever he is—and an answer for you. Are you listening?

She slams down the receiver. The phone begins to ring again. It rings half a dozen times. Finally she picks up the receiver.

Come.

She hangs up.

Scene Two

> *The kitchen, an afternoon in November. BERYL enters, wearing a winter coat and carrying a bag of groceries.*

BERYL: Joanie? Hey, Joanie! Brought you some food. Can you hear me? Bread, eggs, milk—all the boring stuff but listen to this, kid. Mocha fudge almond ice cream! Stacks of red licorice! And...I raided the Catholic church tea. Are you ready for this? Strawberry angel food cake! Chocolate fudge! Peanut butter crisps! Twelve thousand calories, minimum. You may want to share this, hint, hint. Joanie? Are you deaf? I've got your mail too.

> *She reaches in a pocket and draws out letters.*

You won't believe the letters, must be half a dozen. Can you hear me? Letters from Carol-Ann! *(Waits.)* Damn it, Joanie, I'm not going to stand here all winter. I'm going to stand here about two minutes more. Then too bad for you, you'll never find out what I did last night. With handcuffs! *(Waits.)* Aw, come on, Joanie. Think I don't know how bad you feel? Can't we talk about it? We could even talk through the door, if you want. Do you want to? *(Waits.)* All right, kid. Have it your way.

> *BERYL begins to exit as JOANIE enters, in a dressing gown.*

My God. What a mess. Did you hear me? I said what a mess. It's you I'm talking about.

> *The phone begins to ring. BERYL moves to answer it.*

JOANIE: Don't.

BERYL: For heaven's sake—

JOANIE: I've done everything wrong. Everything! All my life.

BERYL: We all make mistakes—

JOANIE: Listen! *(Timed to the rings.)* Dumb...dumb...dumb...

BERYL strides to the phone, picks up the receiver, slams it down.

Dumb.

BERYL: Joanie, for pity's sake.

JOANIE: It rings. And rings...

BERYL: Well, people are worried about you.

JOANIE laughs.

They are!

JOANIE: Don't you know? My number. It's on the wall.

BERYL: What wall. Huh?

JOANIE: At the Drake. In the men's john. Under V.C.

BERYL: What?

JOANIE: V.C. Valued Citizen. Then Joanie. Then the number. Check it out.

BERYL: Honest to God, this town.

JOANIE: Doesn't matter. Brought it on myself.

JOANIE sinks into a chair.

I get a rush of energy and then all of a sudden... Can't sleep, that's why. Can—not—sleep...without dreaming.

BERYL pulls a chair close to her, sits.

BERYL: Joanie, look at me. Look at me! Now listen. I may not be the brightest bulb on the porch—

JOANIE: Don't, Beryl.

BERYL: Don't what.

JOANIE: Say it.

BERYL: Aw, Joanie...

JOANIE: Sshh. Not a word.

            Pause. BERYL rises and moves to the door.

            To anyone.

BERYL: Do me a favour, huh. Don't let that food rot.

            BERYL exits.

Scene Three

            The porch, a few days later. BOONE is at the door. He pounds on it.

BOONE: Joanie! Joanie, open up. It's Boone.

            Lights up fast on the kitchen. JOANIE is at the table, in her nightgown. Her feet are bare. There's a dressing gown tossed across the other chair.

            Joanie? Come on, open up. I want to talk to you.

            JOANIE rises and backs away from the door.

JOANIE: Go away.

BOONE: Joanie!

JOANIE: Go away, go away!

BOONE: I've brought Carol-Ann back. That's what you want, isn't it? Can you hear me?

            At first JOANIE is too stunned to react. Then she moves fearfully to the door.

JOANIE: Where is she?

BOONE: With her grandfather.

JOANIE: She's all right?

BOONE: She's fine. Come on now, let me in.

JOANIE: No.

BOONE: Let me in.

JOANIE: Just send Carol-Ann home and—go away!

BOONE: I can't do that. Now open up, or I swear to God I'll pack Carol-Ann up and take her straight back to Toronto.

JOANIE: If you come in here, I might just kill you.

BOONE: I'm going to count to ten. *(BOONE starts counting.)*

JOANIE: I don't know what you want but I know it's bad, it's got to be awful bad for me!

              BOONE goes on counting. When he gets to ten, there's silence. JOANIE flies to the door and throws it open. Then she steps back. BOONE enters and closes the door.

              Oh, you smell so good. I can smell the fresh air on you!

              This outburst embarrasses her. At the same time, she becomes aware of her appearance. She reaches for her dressing gown, puts it on.

              What are you staring at? Don't you know it's rude to stare.

BOONE: Sorry.

JOANIE: If you'd just phoned ahead, given me a little warning—

BOONE: I tried.

JOANIE: Look at this place, what a mess. Look at me. If I'd known you were coming—

BOONE: It doesn't matter, Joanie. You look about the way I expected you to.

JOANIE: Oh! Do I?

BOONE: I didn't exactly mean that.

JOANIE: I don't know what you expect. You walk in here, out of the blue—

BOONE: All right!

JOANIE moves farther away. When she begins to speak again, the tempo of her speech is erratic, suggesting a struggle to pull herself back to reality.

JOANIE: You're sure she's OK?

BOONE: She's fine.

JOANIE: I can't believe she's here, can't believe you are! Maybe I'm dreaming. Don't look at me like that, it's no dream, I know that. So. She's here. That would be your idea. It wouldn't be Carol-Ann's.

BOONE: She's been worried sick about you. You didn't answer her letters—

JOANIE: I did! Some of them.

BOONE: You wouldn't even pick up the phone.

JOANIE: She's mad at me.

BOONE: I'd say she's resigned—

JOANIE: She's mad.

BOONE: A little. But she's here.

JOANIE: I've got to see her.

BOONE: Later.

JOANIE: I'll call her.

They both move to the phone.

BOONE: First we have to talk.

BOONE takes the phone away.

JOANIE: Talk! About what.

BOONE: Things. But not this way. Calmly, at the table—

JOANIE:	Things!
BOONE:	Like adults...
JOANIE:	All of a sudden we have "Things" to talk about! Well, go ahead—talk. You don't know where to begin, do you? You're maybe better at endings than beginnings.
BOONE:	Oh, I definitely am.

He grins at her for the first time. For him it is a safety valve, but for JOANIE it is like striking a match.

JOANIE:	I want you out of here, now.
BOONE:	Joanie, for God's sake—
JOANIE:	I don't know why you had to come!
BOONE:	I couldn't send her back alone. I had to make sure you were going to be all right.
JOANIE:	Why wouldn't I be?
BOONE:	Come on, Joanie. I know what's been going on. You've had yourself locked up in here—
JOANIE:	You got in, didn't you? So everything's fine. I'm fine! Don't I look just fine?
BOONE:	You want me to tell you how you look?

JOANIE turns away.

I know you've been laid off your job—

JOANIE:	Says who?
BOONE:	Beryl.
JOANIE:	Beryl?
BOONE:	She thinks you can still get it back. If you play your cards right.
JOANIE:	What else did Beryl tell you?

BOONE: Everything, I think. Now listen to me. I'm going to give you some time to sort yourself out. A few days, a week if you need it. If you can pull things together I'll leave Carol-Ann here, but only until she's through school. I want that understood.

JOANIE: Did Beryl—did she say anything about...you know, after Carol-Ann left, there, for a while the house was so quiet I could hardly breathe and I started to...

BOONE: Pick up men.

JOANIE: You didn't tell Carol-Ann.

BOONE: Why would I do that?

JOANIE: I suppose you might as well've, she's going to hear all about it now. Oh...God—oh, I see what's coming, I see exactly what's coming now. She's going to hate me worse than ever.

BOONE: She doesn't hate you, Joanie.

JOANIE: Well, she doesn't like me an awful lot. Takes after her Dad.

            She falters, moves away.

            All this company, all of a sudden. I should get dressed. Wash my hair...

BOONE: It's all gone.

JOANIE: What?

BOONE: Your hair. You cut it all off.

            JOANIE quickly reaches up, touches her hair.

JOANIE: For a minute there, I...

            She sees BOONE watching her.

            What are you waiting for?

BOONE: I want an understanding, about Carol-Ann. When

she's through school, she comes to live with me. And no fuss. Did you hear me?

JOANIE: Maybe you won't want her then.

BOONE: I'll want her.

JOANIE: Maybe she's just another passing interest.

BOONE: I'm a little phobic about permanence, I can't deny that. But with Carol-Ann...it's different.

JOANIE: Is it?

BOONE: For sure. Now listen. Either you agree to let Carol-Ann go—gracefully!—when she's ready, or I'll take her back to Toronto—now, tonight. And no amount of blackmail is going to make me bring her back.

JOANIE: Blackmail! Blackmail, he calls it.

BOONE: There's a better word?

JOANIE: It wasn't blackmail, don't say it was!

BOONE: Call it what you like. It worked, didn't it?

JOANIE: But I never planned it. I never—

BOONE: You don't want Carol-Ann back?

JOANIE: Sure I do, of course! Oh, I can see why you've come. To throw things in my face, see me at my worst—

BOONE: Don't be ridiculous. If she was coming I had to bring her, I couldn't just let her walk in here. God knows how she would have felt.

JOANIE: No. You didn't have to bring her—in person. After all this time. There were lots of other ways to do it. So what did you come for, really?

BOONE: Really? I came for my clothes.

He grins. It is dead quiet for a few seconds, then JOANIE tears into him with both fists flying.

OK, Joanie—

She hits him again. He gets a firm grip on her wrists. She struggles to break away.

Come on, cut it out.

She goes for his face.

Cut it out!

She loses her balance and falls. He tries to help her up but she pulls away.

JOANIE: Don't come near me! Ever! I mean it.

BOONE: *(Very shaken.)* I get the message.

JOANIE: You better.

BOONE: Loud and clear.

JOANIE: *(Rises.)* I said if I let you in I might just kill you and I might! Why shouldn't I? You come stomping in here, cold as ice—

BOONE: I was scared to death.

JOANIE: You weren't scared.

BOONE: You'd know.

JOANIE: You weren't scared, you were mad! I could feel how mad you were clear across the room. I can still feel it! What about me? I'm the one who should be mad. I've got reasons. I've got thirteen years of reasons!

BOONE: Does this mean I don't get my clothes?

JOANIE grabs the closest thing to hand and hurls it at him.

For Pete's sake, you used to have a sense of humour. Look, maybe I should walk out the door and turn around and come in all over again. Should I? Give you time to prepare yourself. Get dressed. Comb your hair. Hang the Welcome Home Banner. *(Grins.)*

| | All right, I was mad. I had to get mad, to get through the door. I'm not mad now. Can I take off my jacket? Or will I still have to make a run for it? |

JOANIE: I'd like to know what you think you've got to be mad about.

BOONE: Would you?

JOANIE: Yes!

BOONIE: Then I'll tell you. You've manipulated us. Backed us into a corner. There were all kinds of sensible things that you could have done—

JOANIE: Sensible!

BOONE: And you didn't do any of them.

JOANIE: Such as?

BOONE: Such as picking up the phone and calling me.

JOANIE: When?

BOONE: In August. The minute she got home. Why didn't you? How am I supposed to know what you're feeling if you won't talk to me?

JOANIE: You should've known.

BOONE: *(Incredulously.)* What?

JOANIE: How I'd feel.

BOONE: Jesus, I'm not a mind reader.

JOANIE: You were once.

BOONE: That's not true. I'll tell you what I knew. Every summer Carol-Ann came down, and every summer she begged to stay. Cried her heart out when I put her on the train—

JOANIE: *(Moving away.)* I won't listen to this.

BOONE: Fine.

JOANIE: I should never have let her go down there, don't know why I did!

BOONE: It was the best thing anyone ever did for me. Joanie? I mean that. *(Pause.)* I'd like to finish what I started to say. Every summer she came down and we—made plans. What we'd do when she came to live there, permanently. I wanted her to know…that I wanted her there. And then finally, last summer, I thought— she'll be coming anyway in a couple of years, why not now? I thought if you didn't like the idea, you'd let me know. That was a reasonable assumption, I thought. Apparently not. Anyway, that's my side of it. Enough said.

JOANIE: I did call. Talked to that—Francesca.

BOONE: You sure did.

JOANIE: And what did you do? Ignored every word.

BOONE: Not true.

JOANIE: Told my own daughter to just—run off!

BOONE: Not true! I told her we'd better reconsider, that's what I told her. I said maybe we should wait a while. And the next thing I knew, she was on my doorstep. I'll admit it made me mad, that phone call. That you'd try to pull that kind of stunt—

JOANIE: I hate it when you talk like that.

BOONE: Like what?

JOANIE: Like I was five years old.

BOONE: I realize now I misunderstood…what was happening around here. OK? Look, maybe we should have a drink or something. Want to do that? What have you got to drink?

JOANIE: Gin.

BOONE: Gin. I'll pass. You?

JOANIE: I hardly ever drink.

BOONE: I remember why. *(He grins. Pause.)* Listen...do you ever sit down?

> *JOANIE makes a big show of obeying him. He takes off his jacket and sits across from her.*

I can't believe you did that to your hair. You once promised me you'd never cut it.

JOANIE: Is that what we're going to talk about? Promises?

BOONE: Good point.

> *A silence.*

JOANIE: You don't look a day older.

BOONE: No?

JOANIE: Well, maybe a day.

BOONE: You've changed.

JOANIE: I've gained some weight.

BOONE: You have.

JOANIE: Just have to glance at food and it winds up on my waistline. No matter how hard I watch it. Watching my waistline—it's like watching history unfold. That's supposed to be funny, that line. It's straight out of the *Reader's Digest*.

BOONE: The last time I saw you, you were skinny as a broomstick. Nothing in your face but eyes.

JOANIE: That's enough about that.

BOONE: You had on a pair of cut-off jeans and sandals. And a little red-and-white striped top—

JOANIE: I never in my life owned a red-striped top.

BOONE: You sure as hell did.

JOANIE: Never.

BOONE: OK, make it yellow. I was standing there, at the door, and you looked up and gave me this big smile...I don't suppose you ever smile, any more.

JOANIE: I don't like talk about my weight.

BOONE: I didn't say it didn't suit you, did I? All that weight. *(Quickly.)* All right! *(Pause.)* Tell me something. Do you think there's a chance in a million we're going to be able to talk to each other without fighting?

JOANIE: I don't know. Part of me's sitting here trying to be nice and part of me's standing over there, egging me on.

BOONE: That doesn't make sense.

JOANIE: Nothing makes sense. I don't make sense, even to myself. Especially to myself. I've been locked up in this house...how long? Listening. For what I don't know. Listening to the phone ring, and stop ringing. People banging at the door, going away. Listening for something that'll make sense out of Joanie! And my mother—you remember about my mother. She keeps coming to see me now, in my dreams. Stands there— big frown! Then turns and goes, walks out the door without a word. Or a backward glance. I keep thinking maybe it's her I'm listening for, maybe she's got an answer for me if I could just come up with the right question!

BOONE: What's happening to you?

JOANIE: I don't know!

BOONE: Maybe I'd better go.

JOANIE: No!

BOONE: You look exhausted.

JOANIE: I'm fine! I'll be fine. It's just—living, you know. I think living has nearly killed me.

              She smiles.

BOONE: *(Meaning the smile.)* There it is, finally.

                He reaches out to touch her—playfully, like he might
                with CAROL-ANN. She grabs his hand.

JOANIE: I always knew someday you'd come back!

BOONE: You knew more than I did, then.

                He tries to pull away.

JOANIE: I never stopped thinking about it! When, and how.
                What I'd be doing when you got here. Not this,
                though—never this! I saw myself—with fresh-
                washed hair, and a pink dress. Remember that pink
                dress I had before we were married, that you liked so
                much? Like that, but new. A new dress, and old
                music playing. Cohen, maybe.

BOONE: Joanie—

JOANIE: And you'd stand at the door for the longest time,
                staring at me. Nobody would move. It would be—
                one of those moments when time freezes… And then
                you'd explain everything. And then you'd stay.

                BOONE manages to get himself free. He leaves the
                table.

                What's the matter? What did I say? I know you're not
                going to stay—don't worry. I do know that! I just
                wish one thing. Wish you didn't have to look so good!

BOONE: Joanie, you know. When I came in that door, and saw
                you, I wanted to…wrap my arms around you and
                hold you—

JOANIE: Never mind!

BOONE: —into next week. *(Beat.)* You're supposed to hate me,
                don't you know that? You get hate and I get guilt,
                that's the way it works. Like two people who wind up
                in the same accident. Different injuries—both
                survive.

JOANIE: *(Not a question.)* How could I hate you.

BOONE: How.

JOANIE: That's what I said—how!

BOONE: Come on, Joanie. I walked.

JOANIE: I know what you did. I just wish you'd told me why.

BOONE: Jesus.

JOANIE: I've been running all the reasons through my head ever since—all the possible reasons. But I still—in all this time I still don't know. I mean, I know…things weren't going so good. You hated it here. Wanted me to quit my job so I did—you asked me to, and I did. Though I notice for some reason you told Carol-Ann—

BOONE: You're not going to start this.

JOANIE: And that day, the day I quit, I took Carol-Ann and waited for you, outside. And the minute I saw you I said Boone, guess what, I quit my job. And you said Good. And gave me a big hug. And kissed Carol-Ann. And then we went inside, like nothing had happened. And after supper, you said—

BOONE: I know what I said.

JOANIE: And you never came back. That's all I know. Sometimes…sometimes I wished you'd died. I did. Couldn't help it. Maybe one of those big machines you were driving at the time rolled and crushed you. That would have ended it, at least. I'd have known where to lay the blame! And then right away I'd hate myself for wishing that. I'd think maybe you couldn't help yourself, maybe you wanted to be content—here, with me—but you just couldn't. You had that curiosity about things, that Carol-Ann's got—that I sure don't have!—and it just…carried you away. You ought to be able to make people content, if you ask me. You ought to be able to—sit 'em down and give 'em a dose of contentment, like cough syrup. Or else, people that are content shouldn't have to get mixed up with people that aren't. But they do—look at me!

Every time I turn around, I'm sitting down at the table with someone who doesn't want to be there. Why is that? How can you enjoy a meal, when nobody else is eating! And then sometimes I turn it all around again. I think maybe if I'd just known why you had to leave, I could've let you go. But I suppose not, I suppose I wouldn't have been ready. I'm never ready! I feel as if my whole life I've been crying out the same two words. Not yet! And nobody ever listens. What's wrong with me? Something's got to be awful wrong with me. Why am I never enough for people?

A silence.

BOONE: What a mess. I wish to God…

He moves abruptly to the table but doesn't sit.

Listen, there's something I want you to know. After Beryl phoned, and told us what was going on here, we sat down and discussed things—Carol-Ann and I. And I left the decision to her. And she chose to come back. Did you hear me?

JOANIE: Chose.

BOONE: I thought you'd like to know that.

He picks up his jacket and puts it on.

I'll send her right over.

JOANIE: What are you doing?

BOONE: Good question. What am I doing? I don't know. I had some notion…crazy. I've had some crazy ideas, but this…

He moves towards the door. JOANIE flies out of her chair and beats him to the door.

Move, Joanie.

JOANIE: No!

BOONE: Move! Please.

JOANIE: Not yet. Not like this.

BOONE: We haven't done anything but fight since I came in
            the door.

JOANIE: No more. Promise.

BOONE: Might as well promise not to breathe.

            BOONE moves away from her.

            You want to dig it up? All that stuff?

JOANIE: Who buried it!

BOONE: *(Beat.)* This is a hell of a lot to put a guy through for a
            box of old clothes.

JOANIE: Clothes!

BOONE: You must have kept them, you kept the sandbox.
            Why on earth did you keep that sandbox?

JOANIE: It goes—first thing next spring. She never used it,
            anyway.

BOONE: I'm not surprised. It was a lousy sandbox.

JOANIE: It was a beautiful sandbox!

            A silence.

BOONE: *(Like a doomed man.)* You want to know why I left? I
            left to save myself.

JOANIE: From what? From me?

BOONE: Yes, all right, from you.

JOANIE: If you'd talked to me, if you'd just once—

BOONE: Joanie—

JOANIE: Talked to me! Instead you shut me out. Took the best
            part of yourself and locked it away. Then once in a

while opened the door a crack and let me peek in. Why? What did I do that was so terrible?

BOONE: Joanie...you're as open as a book, you always were. It's one of the things I liked about you.

JOANIE: Liked!

BOONE: If you're going to quibble with every word—

JOANIE: I bet Francesca just opens that door and walks right in!

BOONE: She doesn't care if she does or not, that's the difference.

JOANIE turns away.

You brought her up. All right—I shut you out. I admit it.

JOANIE: Why?

BOONE: Had to.

JOANIE: Why!

BOONE: I had to have some part of me you couldn't leave teeth-marks on.

JOANIE: You make me sound like—a hyena.

BOONE: You wouldn't leave me alone. I'd go out of the room, you'd follow. Sit in the car, you'd come knocking on the window. I couldn't even take a shower without you poking your nose through the curtain.

JOANIE: Because you kept talking about leaving, that's why!

BOONE: If I was five minutes late, you'd be out on the street, pacing. Pacing! Right up until the very last night. That night, Jesus! Up and down, up and down, up and down. In your cut-off jeans and your red striped top. It was red, Joanie, it's burned into the back of my skull! I turned the corner and saw you and shrank back, and then I started to count. I got to a hundred and I was still shaking.

JOANIE: You've got a funny memory of things—

BOONE: Now you listen to me. Listen! Up until that moment, I really believed that if we could just get out of here, we could make it. But I watched you that night, pacing up and down, and I knew—here or anywhere, I couldn't live with you. With you I was finished. And a little later, after supper, you flashed me a smile— like sun on water. And I walked out the door and down to the station and it happened—it just happened there was a train pulling in. And the track, you know...the next morning when I woke up the train was just taking a curve and the sun glinted on the track and even though I hated myself to the soles of my feet I knew that was it, I'd done it. I'd done the worst thing I could imagine doing...and I'd survived! That's a kind of freedom, you know? After that, you can do anything you have to do.

JOANIE: Just like that. So easy.

BOONE: I didn't say it was easy. I said it taught me something—something I needed to know. That I could do what I had to do to live. (Pause.) But, you know...I've just realized. There's one thing worse than having to do the worst thing you can imagine doing, and that's—

JOANIE: Words!

BOONE: Are you interested in this?

JOANIE: You could always put words together to make things sound pretty. Even ugly things. The uglier the thing, the prettier the words!

BOONE: (Very cool.) Why don't you just tell me what you think I ought to say to you.

JOANIE: What do you mean?

BOONE: Tell me what to say and I'll say it.

JOANIE: What if it isn't true?

BOONE: Maybe I'll say it anyway.

JOANIE: I shouldn't have left. You could say that. Shouldn't have left, don't know why I did!

BOONE: I shouldn't have left.

JOANIE: Like you mean it!

BOONE: *(An explosion.)* Jesus, Joanie, you're a beggar for punishment! All right. You want it, you're going to get it. You say I should have talked to you. About what. Diapers? Dishes? How to make jelly out of goddamn rotten crabapples? What the neighbors were doing, or weren't doing, or would have done if it hadn't rained, snowed, stormed— *(Violently.)* Who cares! Even so, I tried. Hopeless. You wouldn't read a book, not even when I begged you to. An idea, you know—an idea, believe it or not, can be—fucking exciting, a thing of beauty, but you have to share it or it dries up. And you—

JOANIE: I tried. I did! But if I didn't catch on right away you'd turn so cold—

BOONE: That's right. Right again! I didn't have the patience. I couldn't wait, I couldn't sit still. Because the world— oh boy, the world. Is a remarkable place, you know? We were going to see it together, that was the deal—

JOANIE: Before Carol-Ann.

BOONE: Carol-Ann was just a better excuse.

JOANIE: No. I'd have left.

BOONE: You weren't going anywhere.

JOANIE: I quit my job.

BOONE: You weren't going anywhere, and neither was I—if you had to kill yourself to stop me.

JOANIE: *(Turning away.)* I was sleepwalking.

BOONE: Sure, sleepwalking. On the highway, in the middle of the night. In the traffic lane.

JOANIE: I couldn't stand the thought of losing you!

BOONE: I don't know what I was supposed to do. Drive a
                 bulldozer the rest of my life. Go drinking with the
                 boys at the Drake. Dig myself a hole you could pretty
                 up with curtains and wallpaper... You wanted a
                 cocoon. You wanted me to wrap myself around you
                 like a second skin, you thought that would keep you
                 safe, but it wouldn't have. Even if I'd stayed. I never
                 had that kind of power. *(Pause.)* Is that enough? Or do
                 you want more?

JOANIE: I guess you never loved me.

BOONE: Are you listening to me? Have you even heard a word
                 I've said?

JOANIE: Did you.

BOONE: Maybe I didn't love you enough.

JOANIE: You'd say that, you'd have to say that!

BOONE: All right, I loved you too much. What do you want to
                 hear?

JOANIE: I want to hear there's something in the world—one
                 thing only—that doesn't change!

BOONE: Everything changes.

JOANIE: On earth. Only on earth! I can see where I belong.

                 A silence.

BOONE: Christ, what am I doing? I didn't come here to do this.
                 I don't know what you want. If it's answers, I'll give
                 you answers. Have I been happy since I left here?
                 Rarely. Sorry I left? Often. Would I come back?
                 Never. Can I justify what I did? Sometimes. Forgive
                 myself? No. But I'm trying. I think maybe if I can be a
                 decent father to Carol-Ann...

                 *He turns to look at her; she seems lost in a world of her
                 own. He moves to the door and opens it.*

JOANIE: What about the fire? You used to say I was on fire,
               said we both were. Said it was a wonder the sheets
               didn't catch. What about that?

BOONE: I remember that.

JOANIE: Well?

BOONE: Fires go out.

               He exits.

Scene Four

               *The kitchen and porch, the next day. JOANIE sits in
               front of an old trunk, going through the contents.
               BERYL, in a coat, climbs the steps, crosses the porch
               and stops at the kitchen door.*

BERYL: Joanie? It's me. Came to see you.

JOANIE: Hello, Beryl.

               BERYL enters the kitchen.

BERYL: What are you doing?

JOANIE: Going through some old things.

BERYL: You're not mad at me, I hope. Couldn't just sit by and
               do nothing, you know.

JOANIE: I know.

               BERYL takes off her coat, throws it across a chair.

BERYL: Whole town's buzzing—guess that won't surprise
               you. *(Mimics.)* Is that Boone? My God, that's Boone.
               What's Boone doing here? *(In her normal voice.)*
               'Course, nobody's asking him, or Carol-Ann. Or me,
               come to think of it. They just run around asking each
               other.

               JOANIE pulls an infant's sweater from the trunk.

	That's an opening I just gave you. You can pour it all out any time now.
JOANIE:	Look, Beryl. How small.
BERYL:	Aw. She was the cutest little thing.
JOANIE:	She was, wasn't she?

JOANIE studies the sweater.

I think I might let her go, Beryl.

BERYL:	Say that again.
JOANIE:	Might let her go back with her Dad.
BERYL:	Who put that idea in your head? Carol-Ann?
JOANIE:	My mother. It's true. You know all those dreams I've been having—I told you about them. Well, all of a sudden, it started to make sense. Her coming back, after all this time. When I needed her most. Why would she do that, Beryl?
BERYL:	Beats me.
JOANIE:	To show me they never pull free. That's what I think. If I'm dreaming about my mother now, when I haven't seen her in thirty years, don't even know if she's alive—it's because I can't let go of her. So how's Carol-Ann ever going to let go of me? She can't. Even if I send her away, I've got her. Only she doesn't know it yet.
BERYL:	She'll be mad as hell when she figures it out.

BERYL pulls something outrageous from the trunk.

Ha! Get a load of this.

JOANIE puts the sweater back in the trunk, then pulls out a dress.

JOANIE:	You remember this dress, don't you, Beryl?
BERYL:	Could I forget?

JOANIE: This dress. I picked it out of the Simpson-Sears catalogue, sight unseen. Wore it one night only—to my high school grad dance. With a pink corsage that Boone gave me. A month after I wore it, I was married. And a month after that, I was pregnant with Carol-Ann. And you know what, Beryl? I never liked it one bit—this dress. I really hated it, to tell the truth.

          JOANIE begins to rip the dress apart.

BERYL: Stop that.

          JOANIE goes on ripping.

          Well, hell, if you feel that way…

          BERYL begins to rip the dress, too. They start to laugh. When the dress is in pieces, scattered around the room, both suddenly fall silent. In the distance a train whistle sounds.

JOANIE: Listen! You ever been on a train, Beryl?

BERYL: Sure. Once.

JOANIE: I haven't. Or a plane, either. *(With a flash of the old style.)* I have sometimes gotten into a truck. Some people will tell you I've gotten into a few trucks I should've stayed out of.

BERYL: Amen to that.

JOANIE: *(Sinking into a chair.)* Oh, Beryl. What am I going to do?

BERYL: When?

JOANIE: For the rest of my life.

BERYL: Well, kid, I tell you what. We'll do it together. I'll go down with you to the Macleods and we'll get you your job back. That's the first thing. Then we'll go to the Drake and celebrate. *(Quickly.)* No, we won't. We'll go on a diet, that's what we'll do.

JOANIE: Lose weight.

BERYL: Get in shape. Run two miles every morning. Stay out of bars.

JOANIE: Stay out of trucks.

BERYL: Stay out of trouble. Yeah. We'll be good girls. We did it once, we can do it again. *(Long pause.)* But can we stand it?

BERYL falls silent. JOANIE moves to the record player, turns up the music. It is Sam Cooke singing "Bring It On Home To Me."

JOANIE: Beryl? Dance with me?

BERYL turns to JOANIE and, with overdone formality, draws her onto "the floor. " They dance together.

The End.

Beautiful Lake Winnipeg

For Gary

Production Information

Beautiful Lake Winnipeg was first produced at the Manitoba Theatre Centre's Warehouse Theatre in Winnipeg on January 24, 1990, with the following cast:

MITCH .... Robert Bockstael
SALOME .... Rosalie Rudelier
IAN .... David Storch
ALIDA .... Patricia Vanstone

Directed by Larry Desrochers
Set and Costumes Designed by Carole Klemm
Lighting Designed by Hugh Connacher
Original Music Composed by Randolph Peters
Stage Managed by Dianne Domaratzki

The playwright is grateful to the following for their contribution to the development of this play: the Manitoba Arts Council; Manitoba Association of Playwrights; Manitoba Theatre Centre; the members of the 1986-87 Playwrights Unit (PTE/MAP); Playwrights Workshop Montreal (Svetlana Zylin); Larry Desrochers; Gary Hunter; Stephanie Kostiuk; George Toles.

Characters

Scene

A clearing outside a cottage on a remote shore of Lake Winnipeg. Early September.

The cottage is old and quite rundown. It sits at an angle, running from down left to up center. A railed-in porch runs across the front; three steps lead up to it. Under the porch is a crawl space; part of it is enclosed with decrepit lattice-work and part of it is open and used for storage. A wooden door, locked and padlocked, leads off the porch into the cottage. Next to the door is a multi-paned, casement style window, locked from inside. The only piece of furniture is a weathered, wooden picnic table, which stands near the steps.

There are three entrances. One (off right) leads to the lake; the other two run on either side of the cottage, one leading to the cars and to Salome's, the other leading to the barbecue.

Act One

Scene One

Friday, 7:30 p.m. IAN enters. He is loaded down with supplies: a cooler, bags of groceries, overnight bags, etc. Dangling from his teeth is a set of car keys. He almost loses part of his load on entering, steadies himself, moves next to the steps and more or less lets things fall. Then he pockets the keys, glances around the clearing, moves to the table, tests it for strength, does the same with the porch railing. He climbs the steps to the cottage, tries the door and the window; both are locked. He peers through the window into the dark interior of the cottage. Then he leaves the porch, discovers the open crawl space underneath and hauls out a couple of decrepit collapsible chairs. Next he pulls out a lantern and a tin box containing candles and matches, which he spills. He stifles a curse, gathers up the candles and matches and sets them on the table. He rummages through the stuff he carried on and sets out a bottle of liquor, a roll of plastic glasses and a six-pack of beer. He opens a beer, shoves the rest into the cooler. He moves back down right and stares off. A beat. He turns back up-stage. Another beat.

IAN: What the hell am I supposed to do now?

He moves back to the porch, picks up a lounge chair, carries it down right and sets it up. He sits, but the angle of the back is wrong. He stifles another curse. He gets up, adjusts the chair, sits again.

Terrific. No music, no books. Nothing.

He sits staring gloomily off as MITCH enters, tossing a set of keys. IAN turns toward him, waits for him to speak. He doesn't.

Looking for someone?

MITCH: Yeah.

IAN: Who?

MITCH: Alida.

IAN: She's not here.

MITCH: Where is she?

IAN: *(Stands.)* Maybe I can help you. I'm not too familiar with the place, but—

MITCH: Where is she!

IAN: She's out.

MITCH: Out, fuck. 'Til when?

IAN: Look, uh… how would you like to tell me who you are?

MITCH: How would you like to tell me who you are.

IAN: Ian Holden. I'm her fiancé.

MITCH: Her what?

IAN: Her fiancé.

MITCH: *(Grins.)* Her fiancé. No shit.

IAN: And you are—?

MITCH: Mitch, the name's Mitch. I'm her husband.

           An awkward moment for IAN.

IAN: Well! I'm… *(Moves to him, offers his hand.)* Pleased to meet you.

MITCH: Are you?

           A beat. IAN withdraws his hand.

IAN: What, uh… what are you doing here?

MITCH: I could ask you the same question.

IAN: Not really.

MITCH: I just did.

IAN: I'm here with Alida. That should be obvious.

MITCH: Should it?

IAN: I think so.

MITCH: Then where is she?

IAN: I told you, she's out.

MITCH: Out where?

IAN: Look, man I—

MITCH: *(Like a shotgun blast.)* Mitch!

IAN: Sorry?

MITCH: The name is Mitch, didn't I just tell you? Don't call me man. Ever!

IAN: *(Beat.)* Mitch.

MITCH: You got it.

                 MITCH saunters down center.

IAN: I think you should explain why you're here.

MITCH: You do, eh.

IAN: Definitely.

MITCH: All right, I'll explain. I'm here to see Alida. We've got a little business to clear up.

IAN: Business.

MITCH: Yeah, business. How long's she going to be, anyway?

IAN: I don't know.

MITCH: You don't know?

IAN: I don't know. Sorry.

MITCH: Fine. I'll wait.

              He picks up a chair.

IAN: Here?

MITCH: Where else?

IAN: Well, there's a motel down the highway. A café about a mile back.

MITCH: I know that, fuck, you going to draw me a map?

              He carries the chair down center.

IAN: Aw, look, man—

MITCH: *(An explosion.)* Mitch!

IAN: Right, I—

MITCH: Don't make me say it again!

IAN: *(Takes a breath.)* What I was going to suggest— Mitch—is that if you go back to that motel, and wait there, I'll have her call you as soon as she gets back.

MITCH: You will, huh.

IAN: You have my word on it.

MITCH: Yeah? Well your word's worth shit. There's no phone here.

IAN: Well then, I'll drive her over. You go back to that motel, have yourself a cup of coffee, and I'll drive her over the minute she gets back.

              MITCH snaps the chair open.

              I'm asking you to wait somewhere else. No offence.

MITCH: I heard you. *(Sits.)* No offence.

              A beat. IAN laughs uncomfortably.

IAN: You're serious. You really want to do this.

MITCH: Why not?

IAN: It's a bit awkward, wouldn't you say?

MITCH: No.

IAN: No. Well, it's awkward as hell for me.

MITCH: Well then, maybe you should leave.

IAN: I'm here with Alida!

MITCH: Are you? I don't know that, do I?

IAN: What's that supposed to mean?

MITCH: Well, where is she?

IAN: She's out.

MITCH: So you keep telling me but what I'm saying is, how do I know for sure? Maybe you made it up. Maybe you don't even know my wife, maybe you're just some intruder who's set up camp here. I mean, the door's locked, isn't it? How come the door's locked, if you're here with Alida?

IAN: This is crazy, you know that? I don't know whether to laugh, or... (*Trails off, takes a breath.*) You want to know why the door's locked. It's locked because she left in a hurry, and she took the key with her. Okay? She just—she forgot.

MITCH: She must have been in one hell of a hurry.

IAN: Well, as a matter of fact, she was.

MITCH: Why?

IAN: I don't think there's any point in going into that. All I can do is tell you the truth, and the truth is, I'm here with Alida. For the weekend. I'll tell you something else. I don't want to offend you but the last thing she's going to want to see when she gets back here is you.

MITCH: Is that right?

IAN: I'm afraid so.

MITCH: (*Leans in.*) What did you say your name was?

IAN: Ian.

MITCH: Well, listen carefully, Ee-yan. I just spent ninety minutes on the highway—ninety fucking minutes— and I'm not leaving 'til I've seen my wife. Got it? (*Leans back.*) Now. Maybe it's a little unorthodox, this situation we're in here, but it's not catastrophic, is it? Is it!

IAN: No.

MITCH: You can handle it, can't you?

IAN: I think so.

MITCH: You *think* so.

IAN: I can handle it.

MITCH: Good. Then why don't you pull up a chair and sit down and stop worrying about it. Everything's going to be just fine.

            IAN moves to the lounge chair but doesn't sit.

            What's the matter?

IAN: I'll have to ask you not to call her your wife.

MITCH: Are you going to sit down now?

            IAN sits.

            All right?

IAN: Yeah, sure. Fine.

MITCH: Good. So. I take it this is your first time.

IAN: My first—?

MITCH: Time. Here.

IAN: Oh. Well yeah—yeah, it is. As a matter of fact. Alida's been talking about coming up here since the day I met her, but we never quite made it. Until now.

MITCH: So what do you think?

IAN: Well, it—could use some work.

MITCH: I meant the lake.

IAN: The lake? The lake's incredible.

MITCH: You think so?

IAN: It blows me away.

MITCH: No kidding. *(Stares off.)* I hate that fucking lake.

IAN: Really? Why?

MITCH: Everything I once owned is floating in it.

IAN: What do you mean?

MITCH: Alida. Maybe I shouldn't tell you this. It was just before The Big B.U. That's French for break-up. She took everything I owned—clothes, books, photographs, you name it, everything I'd even breathed on. Piled it all up in the back yard and set a match to it. And then—and then! She hired a plane, and flew up here, and dumped all the ashes on Beautiful Lake Winnipeg!

            IAN smiles.

            She did.

IAN: I believe you.

MITCH: And then she sent me the bill for the fucking plane.

            IAN laughs.

            You think that's funny?

IAN: Not for you, I guess.

MITCH: That's for damn sure.

IAN: I imagine she had her reasons.

MITCH: Her what?

IAN: Her reasons, you know, I'm sure she—

MITCH: Look, are you going to tell me now? Or is it still some kind of fucking secret?

IAN: What's that?

MITCH: Where she is!

IAN: She went to see someone. Some woman who lives north of here.

MITCH: Salome?

IAN: That's it, yeah. Salome.

MITCH: Well. In that case, we'd better get ready.

            He stands.

IAN: For what?

MITCH: For a little stormy weather.

IAN: What do you mean?

MITCH: I mean she'll be primed. She'll be flying high on home-made brandy.

            He moves to the table.

IAN: Alida? She doesn't drink brandy.

MITCH: She does with Salome.

IAN: She never drinks brandy.

MITCH: Fine, have it your way. *(Picks up the liquor bottle, examines it.)* Say, Ee-yan. You got anything to drink around here? *(Grins.)*

IAN: Well, sure, obviously, but look, man—

MITCH: *(Slams the bottle down.)* Mitch! Mitch Mitch Mitch! For the last fucking time, don't call me man!

IAN: Why not, man? *(Quickly.)* A joke. It's a joke, all right?

MITCH: You really think you're funny, don't you?

IAN: No, I don't, I... I guess I'm a bit nervous, that's all. I mean, you may be comfortable with this situation but I can't honestly say that I am. Particularly.

MITCH: All the more reason to have a drink. Right?

IAN: There's beer in the cooler.

MITCH: *(Brandishes the bottle.)* I sort of had my eye on this.

IAN: That's not mine, it's Alida's. And I don't think—

MITCH: Good. She owes me. *(Pours a drink.)* You want a beer?

IAN: I've got one. Thanks.

          MITCH *moves back to the chair, sits.*

MITCH: So. Let's see if I've got this straight. You think you're going to marry my wife.

IAN: Your ex-wife.

MITCH: You really think you're going to do it.

IAN: Oh, I'm going to do it.

MITCH: Yeah, right. Does she know about this?

IAN: Of course. We're engaged.

MITCH: Engaged! That's right, you said. When's the big day?

IAN: Well, we haven't exactly—

MITCH: Decided.

IAN: Announced it. But I don't suppose there's any harm in telling you. It's six weeks tomorrow.

MITCH: Six weeks tomorrow. Church wedding?

IAN: A church wedding.

MITCH: Flowers, cake, tuxedo—the whole business?

IAN: Why not?

MITCH: White dress?

IAN: *(Beat.)* You're really subtle, aren't you?

MITCH: It's just a question.

IAN: I don't know.

MITCH: You don't know if she's going to wear a white dress?

IAN: I didn't ask.

MITCH: You should have. That's the kind of question you should definitely ask my wife.

IAN: I asked you to stop calling her that.

MITCH: I mean it. Ee-yan.

              IAN takes a long swallow of beer.

IAN: Okay, it's my turn now, I've got a question for you. How did you know Alida was going to be up here?

MITCH: Why?

IAN: It seems odd to me. We weren't sure, ourselves, whether we'd make it, until just before we left. Did you—drive up on spec, or what?

MITCH: I'll tell you what, Ian. I'll level with you if you level with me. You're not really going to marry her.

IAN: Of course I am.

MITCH: Come off it. You don't have to pull that stuff with me. I know you're screwing her, you don't have to justify it.

IAN: I'm not.

MITCH: You're not screwing her?

IAN: I'm not justifying anything!

IAN stands, moves away.

MITCH: You can't marry her, for fuck's sake. You don't even know her. You've been seeing her, what? A month, two months? A week?

IAN: Six months. Now that's it, man, I mean—I don't mean man, I mean Mitch—Mitch! No more questions, okay? I really mean that. I think if we're going to get along here, until Alida gets back, we're going to have to steer clear of certain subjects, right? Otherwise we're going to end up in trouble, and that would be stupid. Wouldn't it? Pointless. Are you listening to me?

MITCH: Sure, yeah.

IAN: Okay?

MITCH: Whatever you say.

IAN: Good. Okay, good. Great.

IAN picks up his beer, moves down left and sits on the steps. He drinks. MITCH drinks. A beat. MITCH starts to sing a few lines from the song 'Chapel of Love.'

IAN: You're not going to let up, are you.

MITCH sings a few more lines. Then he turns and grins at IAN.

Are you finished?

MITCH: I could be.

IAN: Good. Then maybe you'll answer my question. I asked you how you knew she'd be here.

MITCH: Oh yeah, right. She asked me.

IAN: What do you mean, she asked you?

MITCH: She asked me to come here. For the weekend.

IAN: *(Laughs.)* What is this, some kind of joke?

MITCH: *(Deadly.)* What do you think?

IAN: *(Beat.)* She wouldn't do that.

MITCH: She wouldn't, huh.

IAN: It's completely out of character.

MITCH: Maybe you don't know her so well.

IAN: I know her very well.

MITCH: Do you? I don't think so. I don't think you know fuck-
                all about my wife.

IAN: Look! If you're going to keep talking about her, for
                Christ's sake stop calling her your wife!

MITCH: She is my wife.

IAN: Was!

MITCH: Is. In spirit.

IAN: *(Laughs.)* Amazing. You're amazing, you know that?

MITCH: She thinks so, too.

IAN: Yeah? Well, if she thinks you're so amazing, why do
                you suppose she's decided to marry me?

MITCH: She hasn't.

                IAN stands abruptly, turns away.

                Hey, I'm not trying to offend you. Maybe you think
                she's going to marry you. You probably really think
                that. She's not.

IAN: I can't believe this.

MITCH: Believe it. I know my wife.

IAN: *(An explosion.)* If you don't stop calling her that—

MITCH: I know my wife! And you obviously don't.

IAN: You keep saying that. You've got no business saying
            that. That's an incredible assumption to make.

MITCH: Is it?

IAN: Yes, it is.

MITCH: You think you know her?

IAN: I'm not saying I know everything—

MITCH: No.

IAN: I know as much as I need to know.

MITCH: Yeah? Then you should have known she asked me.
            Right?

            A beat.

IAN: That isn't true, I just don't buy that. If she wanted to
            see you—*if* she wanted to—she'd never do it here.

MITCH: Why not?

IAN: Because—shit! Because she's been talking about this
            frigging weekend for I don't know how long. She's
            been talking about coming up here, where it's nice
            and quiet, where nobody can get at us... She
            wouldn't do it, that's all.

MITCH: She did.

IAN: She wouldn't.

MITCH: *(An explosion, on his feet.)* What's the matter with you,
            fuck, are you deaf, are you dumb? She asked me,
            she's expecting me and here—I—am!

            Stand-off.

IAN: Once you've seen her, you go.

MITCH: Do I.

IAN: Count on it.

MITCH: *(Moves in.)*Aww. I was hoping maybe we could get something going later—the three of us, know what I mean? You up for that?

MITCH reaches out to grope IAN. IAN intercepts his hand and knocks it away.

IAN: There's no limit to you, is there.

MITCH: Aw, loosen up. I'm just trying to pass the time. We've got to pass the time, don't we? What do you want to do, play crib?

IAN moves down right, stares off.

You want a drink? I'll pour.

IAN: No.

MITCH: No! *(Moves to the table.)* You're a lot of fun to be with, you know that? No wonder she asked me along for the weekend.

He pours a drink.

IAN: Look, you know the area. I take it you know the area? Where would I find this Salome?

MITCH: Why?

IAN: I want Alida back here, now. I want this stinking mess cleared up!

MITCH: You've got a boat?

He moves to the lounge chair.

IAN: She took the boat.

MITCH: Then you might as well forget it. You can't get there.

He sits.

IAN: What do you mean, I can't get there.?

MITCH: You can't get there.

IAN: There's no road?

MITCH:	There's no road.
IAN:	Maybe I can walk it.
MITCH:	Nope.
IAN:	Along the shore, maybe.
MITCH:	I'm telling you, you can't get there by land! Got it?

IAN paces.

IAN:	This Salome. Does she have a phone?
MITCH:	Do you?
IAN:	Does she!
MITCH:	No.
IAN:	Are you sure about that?
MITCH:	Nobody up here's got a fucking phone, all right? I'll tell you what you can do. You can swim it.
IAN:	Really?
ITCH:	You can try. Why don't you? Maybe you'll wash up sometime next spring. *(Grins.)*
IAN:	Shit.
MITCH:	Aw, relax, take it easy, she'll be back when she's ready. She'll be back when she's ready!

IAN takes a deep breath, hesitates, then sits.

That's more like it. Now. Why don't we just sit here like a couple of old pals and have a nice juicy chat about my wife.

IAN:	For Christ's sake, man—
MITCH:	Mitch! Mitch Mitch Mitch! What do I have to do, brand it on your forehead?
IAN:	You could always brand it on yours.

MITCH: You little shit—

IAN: What's the big deal, anyway? It's just an expression.

MITCH: Don't use it.

IAN: It's a habit.

MITCH: Break it!

IAN: Are you going to keep doing this?

MITCH: What?

IAN: Squandering all your charm on me.

> *MITCH grins.*

MITCH: If you don't like it, you can always leave. Say! There's a motel down the highway. I'll have her call you.

IAN: Right.

MITCH: Seriously, why don't you?

IAN: Why don't I what?

MITCH: Bugger off.

> *IAN faces MITCH.*

I'm just trying to save you a little embarrassment. I mean, shit., isn't it obvious? You're not wanted here. If she wanted you, she wouldn't have asked me. Right?

IAN: If she asked you.

MITCH: She asked me.

IAN: I'll believe that when I hear it from her.

MITCH: Suit yourself.

IAN: I will.

> *He stands, starts off.*

MITCH: Where are you going now? Up down, up down, fuck. Hey! You had enough? You leaving?

IAN: *(Turns back.)* No, I'm not leaving. I'm going to the car to get my jacket.

MITCH: Good thinking. Bring mine, while you're at it.

          MITCH throws IAN a set of keys.

          I'm parked right next to you.

          IAN starts off.

          Make sure you lock it up again. Fuck.

          IAN exits. For a moment MITCH doesn't move. Then he rises, moves to the table, pours a drink, drains the glass. He moves down right, stares off. IAN returns, wearing an expensive jacket.

          (Meaning the jacket.) Hey, that's the real stuff, isn't it. Class-ee.

          IAN tosses him a light cloth jacket, takes a beer from the cooler and sits on the steps.

          Feel better now? Nice and warm? A little too warm, maybe. Not talking? What are you going to do, sit there and sulk?

IAN: No more talk about Alida. Okay?

MITCH: Like I say, if you don't like it, you can always leave.

IAN: No more talk about Alida! Understand?

MITCH: Yeah, I understand!

IAN: Good.

MITCH: But I'm going to do what I damn well please. I always do what I damn well please. Maybe you know that. Yeah, you probably do, she probably told you. She probably told you plenty.

IAN: Wrong.

MITCH: What do you mean, wrong?

IAN: She doesn't talk about you.

MITCH: Come off it.

IAN: Ever.

MITCH: Yeah? Then tell me this. If she doesn't talk about me, what makes you so sure I'm Mitch?

IAN: *(Beat.)* You said. You walked in here and you said—

MITCH: Where's Alida.

IAN: Where's Alida, I'm Mitch. What can I say, I'm brilliant.

MITCH: Don't get smart , Ee-yan. This is a serious question. Just because I said I was Mitch doesn't mean I am. I could be anyone, a complete stranger. If she never talks about me, how are you going to know?

IAN: Maybe I saw a picture.

MITCH: A picture.

IAN: Yeah, you know, a photograph?

MITCH: She doesn't have one.

IAN: Look, what's the point of this?

MITCH: Maybe she told you what I look like. That's possible. Did she ever tell you what what I look like?

IAN: That would be a little difficult, wouldn't it. Since she never talks about you.

MITCH: Liar.

IAN: What?

MITCH: Fucking liar.

IAN: Watch it, man.

MITCH: Don't call me man!

IAN: Don't call me a liar!

MITCH: How the fuck do you know I'm Mitch!

IAN: *(Beat.)* You know too much.

MITCH: *(Grins.)* Very good, Ee-yan. That's just the answer I was looking for. I know too much! And don't you forget it. *(Moves to the table, lights a candle.)* I know all there is to know about her. All that matters. *(Suggestively.)* Such as where to find her, and how to bring her home.

IAN: Can it.

MITCH: What did I say?

IAN: Don't play dumb. That kind of talk—keep it yourself.

MITCH: Is that a threat? *(Moves to IAN, towers over him.)* I think that's a threat.

          MITCH holds the candle over IAN's head and tips it slightly.

IAN: Knock it off.

MITCH: Are you threatening me? Ee-yan?

IAN: Get away from me, you crazy—

          MITCH tips the candle again; wax drips onto IAN's jacket. IAN knocks the candle out of MITCH's hand, scrambles to his feet.

MITCH: Come on, come on, go for it!

          He shoves IAN.

IAN: Watch it!

          He shoves MITCH.

MITCH: You watch it, punk!

IAN: Asshole!

MITCH: Come on, show me what you got. Show me what you got!

IAN: I will, I'm warning you!

MITCH: I can hardly wait.

            He reaches for IAN's crotch. IAN shoves him.

IAN: Keep your fucking hands off me!

MITCH: Whooo! Scar-ee!

IAN: I want to know what your game is.

MITCH: There's no game, Ee-yan. I'm just trying to keep from getting bored here. I get bored real easy, it's a problem with me.

IAN: No. There's an agenda here, I just can't figure out what it is. I put myself in your shoes—I've been sitting here trying to do that—and I can't imagine, no matter how I felt about Alida, no matter how sore or jealous I might be, I can't imagine doing to anyone what you're doing to me. You're not married to her anymore, you have no claim on her, and no right—absolutely no right—to come prancing in here like you owned the place and start pounding away at me!

MITCH: Ah, don't be such a wimp.

            MITCH moves to the table, picks up the bottle and drinks from it.

IAN: You're an animal, you know that? No wonder you lost her.

MITCH: But I had her. Signed, sealed and delivered. Something you're never going to do.

IAN: That's what this is all about, isn't it. You're trying to scare me off.

MITCH: Awww. You've got it all figured out. Darn it! And it hardly took you any time at all.

He sits.

IAN: You're wasting your time. I'm not going to be driven out of here. I came here with Alida and I'm leaving with Alida. And six weeks from now, I'm going to marry Alida.

MITCH: You wanna lay odds on that?

IAN turns away in frustration.

Hey, I'm serious about this. Fifty bucks. Fifty bucks says you never make it to the altar. Okay?

IAN: No.

IAN moves down right.

MITCH: Thirty, then. How about that? You're scared you'll lose.

IAN: I won't lose.

MITCH: Twenty.

IAN: I can't believe this. Everything is screwed up. From the minute we got here everything has been totally screwed up!

MITCH: Okay then—ten.

IAN: Christ, where is she! It's starting to get dark. How's she going to find her way in the dark? Maybe she's lost.

MITCH: She's not lost.

IAN: She could be.

MITCH: Not a chance. She knows this lake, grew up on it, her daddy was a fucking fisherman.

IAN: I don't like it. Anything could have happened. She could be drifting around out there. I hope she's drifting. I hope she's on the lake, not in it.

MITCH: She's not in the fucking lake, all right?

IAN: We ought to do something.

MITCH: Aw, sit down, you're making me dizzy. There's not a damn thing we can do.

IAN: We can at least worry a bit!

MITCH: You worry. I'll drink. (*Salutes him with the bottle.*) For fuck's sake, would you stop pacing?

              IAN stops pacing. He takes a lungful of air to calm himself.

              Shit. You don't stand a chance, you know that? You'd never make it, even if you did marry her. You don't have the stomach for my wife.

IAN: You don't know me.

MITCH: I know her.

IAN: Yeah, you told me.

MITCH: Inside out. She's not what you'd call uncharted territory.

IAN: Oh, shut up, I've had it up to here with you.

              IAN sits.

MITCH: You don't know what's going on, do you. Still haven't figured it out. (*Leans forward.*) She planned the whole thing. You don't believe me.

IAN: Is there some reason I should?

MITCH: Think about it. First she asks me up here for the weekend, only she doesn't bother mentioning it to you. That's one. Then she asks you here. That's two. Then what? Before you can even dip your big toe in Beautiful Lake Winnipeg, she's disappeared. That's three. You get the picture?

IAN: You're saying she wanted to bring us together. Why?

MITCH: You figure it out.

IAN: She wouldn't do that. She's no sadist.

MITCH: No sadist. Fuck. Are you out to lunch.

            *MITCH stands, goes in search of the lantern, then sets
            about lighting it.*

            I've got a little treat for you, Ian. I'm going to tell you
            a story. Are you listening to this? This goes back, I
            don't know—a year, maybe two years before The Big
            B.U. We were in Florence. You been to Florence?
            Firenze, Italia. Fine city, a very fine city. Not too
            clean, maybe. Anyway, we're there. And Alida's
            flying, she's at the peak of her game. I've never seen
            her so hot. So. One morning I wake up and she's
            gone—no note, nothing. I'm not too concerned. I have
            a pretty good idea where she is. There's a spot we'd
            been to a couple of times, on the river, very... a very
            meaningful spot for both of us. So I pull on some
            clothes and head over there and she's been there, all
            right. She's left her shirt behind.

IAN: Her shirt?

MITCH: Her shirt. So now I know where she's been but I don't
            know where she's gone. All I know is she's running
            through Firenze, Italia half naked.

IAN: You're full of it.

MITCH: Okay, let's say she's not, let's say she's covered up
            like a nun from head to foot. Does that make you feel
            better? I hunt for hours, ask about her everywhere.
            No one has seen her. I mean, they'd remember a
            woman running by with no shirt, right? Finally I start
            checking out the hospitals. That's where I find her—
            in traction, bandages up to here. Cut up bad. You
            want to know what she'd done? She'd run to that spot
            on the river, planning to throw herself in. Started
            taking off her clothes—that explains the shirt, she had
            some idea she wanted to go down naked, I don't
            know. Fortunately, they wouldn't let her jump—a
            dozen people came running—but she managed to
            slip away, across this little square and into a

	building—a bank I think it was, only one story, that was a good thing. Ran up the stairs to the roof, dropped her skirt and jumped. Went right through the roof of the building next door, landed smack in the middle of a barber shop. Brought half the roof down with her. It was glass—did I mention that? The barber shop was a kind of lean-to affair, up against the bank, and the roof was mostly glass.
IAN:	*(Beat.)* Jesus.
MITCH:	You've noticed the scars. You had to notice the scars. She wouldn't tell you how she got them, right? Now you know. *(Sits.)* I'll tell you something. I'd give a lot to have seen the look on that barber's face when she came crashing through.
IAN:	God, you're callous.
MITCH:	Not callous, calloused. I've got callouses in places you don't even know about, thanks to her. *(Drinks.)* What are you staring at?
IAN:	I'm not staring, I'm waiting for the point.
MITCH:	The point.
IAN:	There's got to be a point to the story.
MITCH:	You're kidding me. You don't get it?
IAN:	Why don't you spell it out for me?
MITCH:	The point is she'll eat you alive! Ee-yan.
IAN:	Oh, that's it. A good thing you explained it. I thought you were telling me you'd made her so miserable she wanted to die. She didn't even care how she did it, she was that desperate!
MITCH:	Desperate, my ass. What that was—that whole breath-taking escapade—that's called Living on the Edge. You think you're up for that?
IAN:	It had nothing to do with you, then. You weren't responsible in any way.

MITCH: Of course not.

IAN: I see. Look, I uh... I've got a confession to make. I said Alida never talks about you. That's not true.

MITCH: I knew it. She's always talking about me. She's obsessed with me.

IAN: Yeah. Oh yeah, I'd say so. Like, for instance... one night a few months ago, we were up here on the lake. Not here, of course, south of here. We were at a party, at this house on the beach. A fairly wild party. And after a few hours, we slipped out—went for a walk along the shore. It was something else, I'm telling you. Pitch black, and windy. Waves crashing in but you couldn't really see them, there was just this great—heaving—presence out there, pounding, throbbing... totally out of control, you know? Very sexy. And we uh... I don't know if I should say this but we climbed out onto this huge flat rock that jutted out into the lake—very slippery, very wet—and we... well, we made love there, on that rock, with the waves crashing over us. Every second in danger of being swept off and carried away, and it was—well! I have never been so scared—and so high—in my life.

MITCH: *(Beat.)* Get to the point.

IAN: What's that?

MITCH: Get to the fucking point.

IAN: Right. Well, when it was over, Alida mentioned you. She did, I'll never forget it, she said—you know, Ian. I'd never have jumped through that roof in Florence if Mitch had been half as good as you.

            A deadly silence.

MITCH: You little shit.

IAN: Or maybe she said nice. It's possible she said nice.

MITCH: You fucking little shit.

IAN: You'd still have her if you'd looked after her, don't

you know that? You've got no one to blame but
yourself!

MITCH: I looked after her!

IAN: You looked after her, all right.

MITCH: I looked after her just fine! *(Stands.)* I'm still looking
after her.

IAN: Sometimes she still shakes when she's touched, did
you know that? She can't sleep in the dark, won't
make love in the light. She has nightmares that would
curl your toes. I've even seen her—

MITCH: You think you've got it all figured out, don't you?
Well, I've got news for you. You're just one of a long
line—do you understand what I'm saying? You're
one of a very long line of horny little shits who
thought they were going to save my wife! *(A beat.)*
You don't believe me. You think you're the first.
Come on! A piece like her? Hey, do they still say that?
Do they still call a woman a piece? I'm a little out of
touch.

IAN: Jesus.

MITCH: You're not the first young pup to come sniffing
'round my wife!

            MITCH moves to the table, picks up the liquor bottle.

Now. I've got one last question for you—puppy-dog.
I want to know what you did to my wife.

IAN: What *I* did to her?

MITCH: I think you did her in.

IAN: Did her in? *(Laughs.)* You're nuts, man.

            *MITCH smashes the bottle against the edge of the
            table.*

Christ.

            MITCH advances on IAN. IAN backs off.

MITCH:	Look at it from my point of view. I come all the way up here, expecting to find Alida. Do I find her? No. What do I find? Ee-yan! Sitting here saying the same thing. She's out. Out. *(Swings.)* Out!
IAN:	She is!
MITCH:	Sure she is. Jumped in a boat and took off. Didn't even stop to unlock the cottage.
IAN:	Put that down.
MITCH:	What did you do to her? *(Swings.)* Puppy-dog!
IAN:	You maniac—

MITCH backs IAN up against the cottage and shoves the jagged end of the bottle against his throat.

MITCH:	Talk. Talk, or so help me—
IAN:	She took off in the boat. She was mad and she took off!
MITCH:	She was mad?
IAN:	Yeah, mad. At me!
MITCH:	Why? Talk!
IAN:	We had a fight. In the car, on the way up.
MITCH:	What about!
IAN:	Nothing, just a stupid—a fight, you know? You have them.

MITCH grins.

MITCH:	That's right, puppy-dog. You have them—with her.

MITCH lowers the bottle, steps back.

Fights, scenes, escapades, performances. Games! She needs that stuff, has to have it, she's addicted. You want to spend your life feeding an addiction? Well, do you?

IAN:	At least she'll never bore me.
MITCH:	I know who's going to get bored.
IAN:	I don't think so.
MITCH:	Before you can say puppy-love.

IAN sinks down onto the steps.

What Alida's got, there's no cure for. I'm telling you this for your own good. You think you can cure her but you can't. You know why? Because she doesn't want to be cured. I know. I know because I'm the same, we've got the same—inclination. Maybe you noticed that.

MITCH opens the cooler, takes out a beer.

IAN:	Don't you think you've had enough?
MITCH:	Never enough, puppy-dog. That's my motto.

He toasts him, drinks.

Do yourself a favour, Ian. Get lost. You hear me? Go. While you can.

IAN sits motionless.

You're not going to, are you. Incredible. What are you, stubborn? Or just stupid.

IAN:	Oh, I'm...
MITCH:	What?
IAN:	*(Faces MITCH, hesitates.)* Curious?

They stare at one another. Then IAN stands, moves to a suitcase, pulls out a towel, starts off.

MITCH:	Where are you going.
IAN:	For a swim.
MITCH:	You feel hot?

IAN: No.

MITCH: Dirty?

                MITCH laughs. IAN exits.

                Hey. Hey, Ian! Don't drown.

                Blackout.

Scene Two

                *Twenty minutes later. The clearing is in darkness.
                SALOME sits on the steps, shrouded in shadow. She
                wears a shawl over a flamboyant dress. She holds a
                flashlight at her chest. IAN enters, towelling his hair.*

IAN: Mitch? You there? Who's there?

                *SALOME turns on the flashlight, pointed at her chin,
                and grins ghoulishly.*

                Shit!

                SALOME laughs.

                Shut that off. Would you shut that off?

                SALOME does.

                Who are you?

SALOME: Light the lantern.

IAN: What?

SALOME: The lantern. It's right there by the table. *(Stands.)* Oh,
                never mind, I'll do it.

                She sets the lantern on the table and lights it.

IAN: Are you going to tell me who you are?

SALOME: You don't know me?

IAN: How could I?

SALOME: I know you. Better than you might think. I saw you peeing in the lake. We don't like boys who pee in our lake. Not normally. You just go right ahead and do it.

IAN: Look, who are you, anyway? And where's Mitch?

SALOME: Mitch?

IAN: Yeah, Mitch. Do you know him? He was just here.

SALOME: Right. (*Draws a flask from her pocket, uncaps it.*) I suppose you're going to want some. It's good, made it myself. It's brandy.

IAN: Salome! You're Salome, aren't you?

SALOME: (*Sings.*) 'Salome, oh Salome, 'At's my girl, Salome.'

IAN: Oh boy, am I glad to see you.

SALOME: 'Standin' there with her bum half bare, Every little wiggle makes the boys despair.'

IAN: Listen—

SALOME: "Every little wiggle makes the boys despair!"

IAN: (*Beat.*) I need to know where Alida is.

SALOME: (*Turns away.*) No kidding.

IAN: She took off in the boat—fifty, sixty minutes ago. She was headed for your place, but you—oh God. You haven't seen her.

SALOME: Says who?

IAN: Tonight? You've seen her tonight?

SALOME: I've seen her. And you've seen Mitch, right?

IAN: Right.

SALOME: Right! (*Leans into him.*) Mitch is a dead man. Murdered. Maybe you'll be a suspect, we could use a few of those. (*With overdone authority.*) Who are you, anyway? What are you doing here? Where's Alida?

IAN:	That's what I want to know! Now listen to me, listen! Did she make it to your place?
SALOME:	She lands on her feet. Like a cat.
IAN:	Then she made it.
SALOME:	She made it.
IAN:	Thank God. Then where is she now? Where is she!
SALOME:	Don't shout at me. How the hell do I know where she is?
IAN:	You were just with her! Weren't you just with her?
SALOME:	I was just with her.
IAN:	Well then?
SALOME:	I have no idea. *(Offers the flask.)* Want a nip?

IAN spins away in frustration.

I said do you want a nip.

IAN:	No.
SALOME:	No! Rude boy.
IAN:	What is going on around here, would somebody please tell me? *(Spins back.)* How did you get here?
SALOME:	I walked.
IAN:	You walked. He said you couldn't walk it. He said there was absolutely no way to get from your place to here by land.
SALOME:	Who did?
IAN:	Mitch!
SALOME:	Well, if you're going to talk to dead men... *(Adjusts her dress.)* Tell me something, do you like my dress? It's not too much. is it?
IAN:	*(Turns away.)* Incredible.

SALOME: Do you like it or not?

IAN: Forget about your dress and think about Alida!

SALOME: What about her?

IAN: Where is she?

            ALIDA has entered. Over her clothes is a life jacket.

ALIDA: I'm right here.

            IAN spins around to face her.

            And I'm in trouble.

IAN: I want to know where you've been.

ALIDA: I've been at Salome's.

IAN: All this time?

ALIDA: No. I've spent most of the time sitting out on that damn lake, rowing. I ran out of gas, can you believe it?

IAN: Alida…I've been worried about you.

ALIDA: Well, you shouldn't have been. I keep telling you I'm too evil to die young.

IAN: No jokes, Alida. I'm in no mood for jokes.

ALIDA: All right. What do you want me to say, that I'm sorry? I'm sorry. I behaved badly. Ran off and abandoned you, your first night here. But I'm back now. So. Why don't you come over here and… make me feel welcome?

            IAN moves to her but doesn't touch her.

            What's the matter.

IAN: You've been drinking.

ALIDA: A little brandy.

IAN: I thought you hated brandy.

ALIDA:	Don't do this, Ian. Don't spoil what's left of the evening.
	He kisses her.
SALOMIE:	Are we going to eat or what?
ALIDA:	*(To IAN.)* Your lips are cold. You've been swimming.
IAN:	Yes. *(Unbuckles her life jacket.)* I went for a swim, and I thought about things, and I decided to give you the benefit of the doubt.
ALIDA:	I beg your pardon?
IAN:	*(Removes the life jacket.)* Ask her to leave.
SALOME:	What's that?
IAN:	Ask her to leave, Alida.
ALIDA:	I can't do that. I told her we'd feed her.
SALOME:	Damn right.
IAN:	I mean it, Alida.
ALIDA:	What's the matter with you? I can't send her home hungry. If you could see what's in her fridge—
IAN:	*(Takes her by the shoulders.)* Listen to me! We have to talk, it's important.
ALIDA:	You're shaking. Why are you shaking?
IAN:	*(Lets go of her.)* Jesus, Alida! I thought you were out there on the lake, all this time, or in it, or washed up on shore somewhere—
ALIDA:	I'm fine, feel me. I'm real!
IAN:	And this place. I hate to have to tell you, this is some secluded hide-away.
ALIDA:	Oh well, Salome.
IAN:	I'm not talking about Salome. I'm talking about Mitch.

ALIDA:	*(Beat.)* Mitch.
IAN:	Your charming Ex. He was here.
ALIDA:	That isn't funny, Ian.
IAN:	I didn't think it was. Especially when he smashed the whiskey bottle and went for my throat.
ALIDA:	*(Backs off.)* There's something in the air tonight, can you smell it? Lunacy!

She runs up the steps to the door.

IAN:	Did you hear what I said!
ALIDA:	*(Searches her pockets.)* Oh hell, I've lost the keys.
SALOME:	Does that mean we don't get to eat?,
ALIDA:	Damn it anyway. *(Rattles the door, moves to the window, rattles the window.)* Wouldn't you know it? Everything's locked up tight.
IAN:	Alida—
ALIDA:	Never mind, I'll think of something. But first I need a drink. *(Moves down the steps to the table, picks up the broken bottle.)* My whiskey. *(Faces IAN.)* Is this what's left of my whiskey?
IAN:	I just finished telling you—
ALIDA:	Ian! A brand new bottle.
IAN:	If it makes you feel any better, he drank it first.
ALIDA:	Who did?
IAN:	Mitch! *(Moves to her, takes the bottle.)* Now listen to me, listen! We have to talk about this.
SALOME:	I say we eat first.
IAN:	Butt out, Salome.
SALOME:	You butt out!

IAN: *(To ALIDA.)* We have to talk about Mitch!

SALOME: Mitch is dead! I told you that already, what's the matter with you, don't you understand plain English?

                A beat.

ALIDA: He is. *(With a strange little laugh.)* He's dead.

SALOME: He was murdered.

ALIDA: He wasn't murdered

SALOME: He was murdered.

ALIDA: He drowned. Out there. Four years ago. So I don't know who was here but it wasn't Mitch, was it?

                She moves away.

IAN: You never told me he was dead.

ALIDA: No?

IAN: No.

ALIDA: Well, I suppose you never asked.

IAN: It's not the sort of thing you ask, it's the sort of thing people volunteer.

ALIDA: Do they.

IAN: They do, yeah. They mention it, in passing.

ALIDA: But I never talk about him, you know that.

IAN: Alida, for Christ's sake—

ALIDA: I know. You don't think it's true, but why not? People die all the time, why not him? He could have.

IAN: All right. How?

ALIDA: I told you, he drowned.

IAN: How?

ALIDA: How do people usually drown?

IAN: *(A warning.)* Alida—

ALIDA: All right! He was fishing. He was out there, alone, in a boat, fishing, and... something happened.

IAN: What?

ALIDA: He was alone in the boat! *(Sits.)* It was just at breakup, when the water is—mercifully cold. He would have died the second he hit the water, and then he'd have gone out with the ice. Who knows how far he got—Hudson Bay, Baffin Bay, Iceland. So that was good, he always liked to travel. A joke, Gloompot.

SALOME: The boat washed up north of here. Without oars.

ALIDA: Salome—

SALOME: I don't care, I'm suspicious.

ALIDA: Well, anyway. That's how he went. Lake Winnipeg got him, and I say good for Lake Winnipeg.

IAN: *(Trying to stay cool.)* Why are you doing this?

ALIDA: You asked me, you wanted to know.

IAN: You're pulling that stuff again—flying off into fantasyland! I'm telling you, Alida, this is no time for that.

ALIDA: If you don't like it then for God's sake stop talking to me about Mitch!

IAN: Listen to me. You can't just pretend it didn't happen, I'm not going to let you do that. He was here—

ALIDA: No.

IAN: He was here, with me, tonight. Now that's a fact, you can't wish it away. And, Alida, you know what he said? He said that you'd—

ALIDA: I won't listen to this! I've been on the lake for nearly an hour—rowing in the dark—and I'm sick of my own thoughts and I'm starving! I don't suppose you thought to start the barbecue.

IAN: The barbecue.

ALIDA: It didn't occur to you I might be a little hungry when I got back?

IAN: I've had other things on my mind.

ALIDA: Obviously.

IAN: Are we going to fight about this now?

ALIDA: Not if you do as you're told!

IAN hurls the broken bottle against the cottage.

SALOME: Hey! Watch it.

IAN: *(To ALIDA.)* You've got ten seconds.

ALIDA: *(Beat.)* Yes, all right. He's not dead.

SALOME: Alida!

ALIDA: He's not, Salome.

SALOME: Since when?

ALIDA: *(To IAN.)* It's just a story we invented, because I wanted him dead so badly. I wished him dead, I willed him dead… and one day he was.

SALOME: What are you saying?

ALIDA: We extinguished him, Salome, remember? *(Touches her temple.)* Up here. What a relief. To have one small place in the world where he didn't exist.

SALOME: I don't get this. I don't get this at all.

ALIDA: Ignore her, she's plastered.

SALOME: Liar.

ALIDA: That's enough out of you. I think you'd better go home.

SALOME: Without eating?

ALIDA: We're locked out, Salome.

SALOME: Well—can't we break in?

ALIDA: No, we can't break in! We've got to find the keys. Maybe you can do that. Can you look for them?

SALOME: Where?

ALIDA: The boat. Check the boat, and all along the path to the dock. Take your flashlight. *(Sweet reason.)* If you find them, then we can eat.

SALOME: I don't see why I have to do all the grub work.

                  SALOME exits, with the flashlight.

ALIDA: I wish you wouldn't look at me like that.

IAN: Like what.

ALIDA: Like you don't know whether to hug me or hit me.

IAN: I don't understand you. I don't understand why you'd try to pretend the guy is dead.

ALIDA: She started it. She started saying he was dead and I just… *(Catches herself.)* Right. Sorry. It was wishful thinking. When it comes to Mitch, I do a lot of that. Is that so terrible? Oh, God. He was really here, wasn't he. Why?

IAN: He said you'd invited him.

ALIDA: He would.

IAN: You didn't?

ALIDA: *(Faces him.)* I beg your pardon?

IAN: Reassure me.

ALIDA: I will not.

IAN: Thanks.

ALIDA: I'm not going to play into his hand.

IAN: Forget him, it's me you're dealing with here!

ALIDA: I won't play into yours either. You don't deserve it, you're as bad as he is.

IAN: *(Sighs.)* Alida—I didn't really believe him.

ALIDA: You sure as hell did, it's written all over you.

IAN: *(An explosion.)* I'm still here, aren't I! Now I told you when you got back, when you finally got back here what did I say to you? *(Moves to her, takes her arms.)* I said I'd gone for a swim and thought about things, and I'd decided to give you the benefit of the doubt.

ALIDA: That's supposed to make me feel better?!

                IAN lets go of her, turns away.

                Why would I invite him, for heaven's sake? What reason would I have? What reason did he give?

IAN: Business.

ALIDA: Business?

IAN: First he said something about some business that had to be cleared up. And then later he…implied that you wanted me to meet him.

ALIDA: You must be joking.

IAN: He went to quite a bit of trouble to convince me that marrying you would be an adventure about on a par with swallowing cyanide.

ALIDA: Oh I get it. I'm starting to get the picture now. He's been telling you stories, hasn't he. Filling your ears with fantasies! What did he tell you? No, let me guess. Florence! He told you about Florence, didn't he. How I went running through Firenze, Italia stark naked—or did he allow me a skirt, it varies—and jumped through a roof and scarred myself in several significant places. Did he tell you about that? Of course. It's easily his most engrossing lie. But you believed him.

IAN: Not exactly.

ALIDA: What does that mean!

IAN: I believe it happened. Not the way he tells it.

ALIDA: You think I go around jumping off roofs.

IAN: You've got the scars to prove it.

ALIDA: I've got scars, what does that prove?

IAN: Then you didn't jump off a roof?

ALIDA: There you go again! *(Moves to the table, slams fist down.)* Oh, what I wouldn't give for a drink!

            ALIDA gets herself in hand.

            Don't you see what he was trying to do?

IAN: Oh, I see it, I think. The question is, why.

ALIDA: Who knows. Maybe he was bored. When he was a boy—now this is a true story. His father was a cop, and when Mitch was a boy, he used to sneak his father's revolver out of the holster and run off to some park with it, and put one bullet in the chamber and point the gun here— *(Points a finger at her temple.)* —and pull the trigger. He did! Often. Do you know how he explained that kind of behaviour? He said he was so bored with life that he needed the possibility of dying to keep from killing himself. That's what he said, you figure it out. And there's something else. He's terribly possessive, always was. He's never really got it through his head that I'm not his any more. He's obsessed with me.

IAN: That's funny. He said the same thing about you.

ALIDA: And what do you think. Am I?

IAN: I hope not, Alida.

ALIDA:	*(Beat.)* No one could accuse you of dishonesty.
	She turns away. Silence.
IAN:	Look, I don't want to fight about it anymore. You know how I feel about you—
ALIDA:	How do you feel about me? Tell me, I need to know.
IAN:	I'm going to marry you, aren't I?
ALIDA:	I make you crazy. I make you so crazy, you'd like to crush me. Say it.
IAN:	You make me crazy.
ALIDA:	Do you love me?
IAN:	Yes.
ALIDA:	Trust me?
IAN:	In what way? *(Beat.)* Okay, I don't completely trust you. So what. I made that trade-off months ago. Don't look at me like that, you know what I'm talking about. I *had* someone I trusted completely, and I left her, didn't I. I left her for you, Alida.
ALIDA:	*(Moves to him.)* Oh, Ian. Sweetheart. Don't let him come between us. Please.
IAN:	All right. *(Kisses her.)* I'm sorry.
ALIDA:	That's not sorry. This is sorry.
	She kisses him seductively. SALOME enters, with an axe.
SALOME:	Whore.
	ALIDA and IAN pull apart.
ALIDA:	Back already. Did you find them? You forgot to look.
SALOME:	No, I didn't forget to look. They're not there. *(Hoists the axe.)* But anyway, I got this.

ALIDA: What for?

SALOME: We're going to break down that door.

ALIDA: No, we're not.

SALOME: We sure as hell are.

ALIDA: Nobody's taking an axe to my cottage! Do you hear me?

              ALIDA strides to SALOME and grabs the axe.

              Do you?

              SALOME shrugs. ALIDA turns to IAN.

              I'll be right back.

              She starts off.

IAN: Where are you going?

ALIDA: To find my keys.

IAN: No, you're not. You're not going anywhere while he's around.

ALIDA: What are you talking about? He must be gone by now.

IAN: I'm afraid not. *(Draws MITCH's keys from a pocket.)* I've got the keys to his truck. So I don't know where he is but he hasn't gone far.

ALIDA: I see. *(Rallies.)* Well—too bad!

              She starts off. IAN catches her.

IAN: Alida, just a minute. I don't want you wandering around out there in the dark.

ALIDA: I'll take the flashlight.

IAN: That's not the point. I'll go.

ALIDA: You don't know the way.

IAN:	We'll both go.
ALIDA:	What do you think he's going to do—creep up behind me and murder me? If he didn't do that in eight years of marriage, he's not going to do it now. Besides. I'm kind of handy with an axe.
IAN:	I don't know how you can joke about this.
ALIDA:	We have to find the keys, Ian.
IAN:	Maybe we should just clear out. Go back to town.
ALIDA:	If we did, we'd be playing right into his hand. We can't do that. We've got to show him he can't get to us. That's the only way we can beat him.
IAN:	I suppose.
ALIDA:	If it makes you feel better, I'll take Salome with me. In the meantime, know what you can do? Make a hungry girl happy. *(Kisses him.)* Start the barbecue.
IAN:	*(Reluctantly.)* Where is it?
ALIDA:	Back of the cottage. Go, Gloompot.
IAN:	How long will you be?
ALIDA:	Ten minutes.

IAN exits. ALIDA turns to SALOME.

What's the meaning of this?

SALOME:	Of what?
ALIDA:	*(Indicating the axe.)* A bit obvious, don't you think?

SALOME shrugs.

Okay, give it here.

SALOME:	What?
ALIDA:	The brandy, Salome. Come on, you're already three sheets to the wind.

SALOME: That's a lie.

               ALIDA grabs the flask.

               Let go. Let go or I'll scream!

ALIDA: *(Lets go, stands back.)* That does it. You're finished.

               ALIDA picks up the flashlight and starts off.

SALOME: What do you mean, finished?

ALIDA: *(Turns back.)* Finished.

SALOME: No, I'm not. I don't like the way you treat me, that's
               all. I'm not dirt under your feet. And I don't like being
               the one who's stupid and dispensable and—sexless!

ALIDA: You're finished.

SALOME: Now? This minute?

ALIDA: Of course not. You've got work to do. And Salome...
               (Draws a nail file from her pocket and leans in.) Do you
               see this?

SALOME: I'm not blind.

ALIDA: What is it?

SALOME: A nail file.

ALIDA: Spoil this for me, and I'll ram it up your nose.
               Remember that.

               *ALIDA pockets the nail file and exits, with the axe and
               the flashlight.*

SALOME: Ram it up your own nose. Whore.

               SALOME drinks.

               Blackout.

Scene Three

> *Twenty minutes later. IAN sits in the lounge chair, lost in thought; his thoughts aren't pleasant. Neither are SALOME's. She's on the steps, with her flask. Finally, IAN rouses himself, checks his watch.*

IAN: She should be back. She should have been back ten minutes ago.

> *IAN stands, moves down right, takes a deep breath, stares off.*

God, this place is really something, isn't it. This lake. *(Looks up at the sky.)* Look, Salome. The gods are showering.

> *SALOME scowls.*

I know what you think. You think that's Northern Lights, but you're wrong. The gods are showering, behind their luminescent shower curtains.

> *No response. He faces her.*

How come so quiet? You can talk to me, you know. They can't hear. How can they hear when they're showering?

> *He smiles. She turns away. He moves to the steps and sits next to her.*

Look, Salome, I'm sorry. I thought you were going with Alida, I was counting on that, and when I came back and you were still here, I just—I guess I exploded. I shouldn't have done that. Will you accept my apology?

> *SALOME shrugs.*

Good. Because I don't see any reason why you and I can't be friends.

SALOME: *(Beat.)* You want to be friends.

IAN: That's right.

SALOME: With me.

IAN: Well, sure.

SALOME: I'm sorry to disappoint you but I don't want a friend. I'll tell you what I do want. I want a lover. Wanna be my lover, lover?

IAN: What is this?

SALOME: A proposal.

IAN: I'm already engaged.

SALOME: A proposition.

IAN: Come on, this is crazy talk.

SALOME: Look, I don't have all night. Are you game or not?

IAN: Not.

SALOME: Fine. *(Stands.)* Then don't come wheedling around me, talking about shower curtains in the sky and grinning that silly grin, because it won't do you a bit of good. I wasn't born yesterday. I know what you want from me, and it's not friendship.

IAN: *(Beat.)* Okay, maybe you're right. Maybe I am after something here—a little help. I thought, since you're a friend of Alida's—

SALOME: I'm not her friend. And even if I was, what makes you think I'd want to help you? Why should I? What are you going to do for me, if I do? Huh?

IAN: Not much, I guess.

SALOME: Right. Story of my life.

                 SALOME moves to the lawn chair, sits.

                 I don't know what you see in her, anyway. I don't know what anyone sees in her.

IAN: You don't know her, I guess.

SALOME:	I know her! Like a daughter. I raised her.
IAN:	You raised her.
SALOME:	That's what I said.
IAN:	What about her father? Where was he while you were raising Alida?
SALOME:	As far away as we could keep him.
IAN:	No, see—that's not right. I know it's not right because I know about her father, that's one person she's always talked about. She's always said how close they were, how—
SALOME:	Close?
IAN:	—she'd—run down to shore every day after school, to watch for his boat. And the minute she'd see it, she'd—run straight home, to fix his supper—
SALOME:	She told you that? She lied. She couldn't even peel a spud 'til she was twenty. And she didn't watch for him not once, I can tell you that. I'm the one who raised her, and I'll tell you something. She was a horrible kid.
IAN:	Here we go.
SALOME:	She was horrible!
IAN:	Alida's right, there's something in the air tonight.
SALOME:	You know what kind of kid she was? I'll tell you. The kind that cuts worms in half and feeds the pieces to babies. And snips the nipples off kittens to see if they'll bleed. I mean it. And one time—this was the year the lake was so low. She spent three days catching frogs, you know why? So she could run spikes through them and chart how long it took them to die!
IAN:	What is it about this place? Everybody's got some kind of sick, twisted story to tell about the person who just left!

SALOME: You don't believe me. You will.

IAN: If you know her so well, I guess you know about her scars.

SALOMIE: What about them?

IAN: I guess you know how she got them. Come on, you raised her. Like a daughter!

SALOME: I know, don't worry.

IAN: I wonder. *(He moves to her.)* Here's another question for you. Listen carefully. If a person runs out of gas between your place and here, and has to row back, and if it takes nearly an hour to do it, how far is it from your place to here? Come on, Salome, you know the answer.

        Silence. He turns away.

        Never mind, I know it, too. What I don't know is this. Why would a person spend nearly an hour rowing between your place and here, when they could walk it in a few minutes? No, that's not the question. The question is, why would a person say they'd spent nearly an hour rowing—in the dark—to get from your place to here, when it couldn't possibly be true? You see, Salome, I don't know what's going on around here but I sure know something is. If you'd help me—give me one little clue—I could take it from there.

SALOME: Stuff it.

IAN: Stuff it. Great. I'm in your debt forever.

        IAN steps back, checks his watch.

        Half an hour. That's it, we're going after her.

SALOME: Forget it.

IAN: Come on. I'll drag you if I have to.

SALOME: Don't you touch me.

IAN: I need you to show me the way, Salome. Aw, don't do this, don't make me force you.

SALOME: I'd like to see you force me. I'd like to see you try!

IAN grabs SALOME and begins to haul her off.

Let go! Let go of me! Goddamnit, why don't you just do what you're supposed to do!

IAN: And what's that?

SALOME: Wait here! That's the way she set it up, that's how she wants it to go. So why don 't you stop whining about it and let it happen the way it's supposed to happen!

IAN lets go of her.

IAN: Oh God. Oh God, Salome, don't say that. I was— hoping...

SALOME: Yeah, well, I don't care, I don't give a darn. Serves her right. Serves you right, too. If you'd just make yourself useful! For instance there's supper. God knows, we've waited long enough for a bit of food. Why don't you look after that, huh? You're not going to, are you. Of course not. I can see who's going to have to do it—me! As usual. *(Moves to the table rummages through the bags.)* Or listen to her whine about her stomach. If there's one thing I can't stand, it's people whining about their stomachs!

The rummaging becomes an exercise in futility. She sinks down onto the steps.

That bit I mentioned, about the frogs? She didn't do that. It was me, did that. Okay? It was me. *(Laughs.)* What a brat. I'm not stupid, though. Are you listening to me? Maybe I act like I am, but I'm not. I'm a lot smarter than her.

Suddenly ALIDA stumbles on, covered with blood. She carries the axe and a bottle of wine.

ALIDA: Ian?

IAN: My God.

ALIDA: Look at me, what a mess. *(A strange laugh.)* Ian? Sweetheart?

                 Three beats.

                 Blackout.

                 End of Act One.

Act Two

Scene One

> *Half and hour later. Moonlight, crickets, etc. Another lantern and various candles have been lit. ALIDA sits in the lawn chair, wearing a terry-cloth robe and a towel around her head. IAN enters, carrying a barbecue fork and a steak on a paper plate. He tosses the fork on the table, moves to ALIDA and hands her the plate.*

ALIDA: That's it? Meat?

> *IAN stares at her until her glance shifts.*

If it's the best you can do. *(Takes the plate.)* Aren't you having any?

IAN: I've lost my appetite.

ALIDA: I'll need a knife and fork.

IAN: Oh? Why?

ALIDA: Very funny. What are you staring at?

IAN: I've never seen a murderer before. An axe murderer, to boot.

ALIDA: Well? How do I look?

IAN: Fraudulent.

> *ALIDA stands abruptly, moves to the table, rummages.*

ALIDA: Damn. Every damn thing's locked up inside.

IAN: Too bad you didn't find the keys.

ALIDA:　　That's for sure.

IAN:　　Did you look?

ALIDA:　　Of course I looked.

IAN:　　Before or after you hacked him up?

ALIDA:　　I don't remember.

IAN:　　I'll bet you don't.

> *ALIDA picks up the barbecue fork, weighs it, drops it, then tosses the plate on the table.*

ALIDA:　　I guess I've lost mine, too.

IAN:　　*(Deadly.)* Eat it.

ALIDA:　　I beg your pardon?

IAN:　　Eat it or I'll shove it down your throat.

ALIDA:　　I'm not hungry!

IAN:　　*(Moves to her.)* Oh yes, you are, you're starving, you've been crying for your supper all night long. *(Picks up the steak, shoves it under her nose.)* Well, I cooked it. Just the way you like it, see? See the blood oozing from the center? Now you—eat it!

> *ALIDA knocks the plate out of his hand.*

　　Alida, so help me—

ALIDA:　　What a shame. There's blood all over your nice designer clothes.

IAN:　　If you don't start levelling with me—

ALIDA:　　I am leveling with you!

IAN:　　Good. *(Grabs her hand.)* In that case, there's a body, right?

> *He begins to pull her off.*

ALIDA:　　What are you doing?

IAN:	We're going to find it.
ALIDA:	No!
IAN:	Yes!
ALIDA:	No! No, Ian I can't go back there! Ian!

ALIDA breaks free.

Stop staring at me. I can't go back and look at him. For God's sake, what do you think I'm made of?

IAN: I don't know, Alida. I'm really beginning to wonder.

Ian moves to the lawn chair and sits. ALIDA rips the towel from her hair—which is damp—and tosses it aside.

ALIDA: I must say I'm disappointed. I think, after what I've been through, I deserve a little sympathy. *(Shudders.)* What's the matter with me, can't seem to stop shaking. *(Turns back to the table, picks up the wine bottle.)* Where did this come from? My God! I brought it with me, didn't I? From Salome's. But when did I pick it up? Before? After? Strange, I can't remember a thing.

She picks up a corkscrew, begins to uncork the wine. Suddenly, she stops.

Yes, I can! I can remember the look on his face when I hit him. So surprised! There were words just forming on his lips...lost forever. Well. They probably all started with "f," anyway.

She glances at IAN, then crosses to him with the wine and the corkscrew.

Ian? Gloompot? Would you do the honours?

IAN: A woman who can kill a man with an axe ought to be able to open her own wine.

ALIDA: I'd rather you did it for me.

IAN:	Or maybe I've got that wrong. Maybe you didn't kill him, maybe he was already dead. Maybe he drowned, in Beautiful Lake Winnipeg! Took the underwater route to Iceland.
ALIDA:	You're being bitchy. It doesn't suit you.
IAN:	No, wait a minute. That's wrong too, that's just wishful thinking. He didn't drown, he's alive and well. Charming as ever! He damn near charmed the pants off me—did I mention that yet? Oh yeah, take it from me, the man can perform. Question is, what was the point? What exactly was the point of the performance, and where is he now? I'd like to know that, too, because I've got the keys to his truck and I'm starting to think they'd look real good tangled up around his tonsils!
ALIDA:	You're not going to, are you.
IAN:	I'm going to try!
ALIDA:	I meant the wine, silly.

IAN grabs the wine, leaps to his feet, prepares to throw the wine violently off right, but ALIDA grabs his arm.

No, no, no, not the wine! Ian!

He lets her pull the wine from his hand.

You'd like it to be me, wouldn't you? You'd like to pick me up and hurl me against the rocks, smash me to pieces. Maybe before the night's out, you'll do that. Will you? (*Moves in tight.*) If you do, if you decide to dash my brains out on those rocks over there, you know what? I'll understand. In that split second before my skull cracks open, I'll know the emotion that drove you to it. And in a funny kind of way, I'll rejoice. Because I'll know we were meant for each other.

Five beats. Nobody moves.

IAN:	You're a monster.

ALIDA: That's not what you said last night. In the dark, between the sheets. Remember?

IAN moves abruptly away.

Now you act as though I'm diseased—liable to contaminate you. It's not fair. I did it for you, Ian.

IAN: Did what, exactly?

ALIDA: Killed him!

IAN: You shouldn't have bothered.

ALIDA: That's right! I remember now! It was for you. It was you we were fighting about! I opened the door and he—loomed up, out of the shadows. For a split second, I didn't recognize him at all. And then immediately, automatically, we began to fight. He wouldn't back down, would not back down. I ran outside, he followed. And then, out of the blue, it hit me: I am tired—bone tired—of fighting with this man. And in the same second I felt the weight of the axe in my hand and so I... swung it. So natural, so easy, like falling into bed.

IAN strides across to her and takes the bottle from her hand.

IAN: Okay, you've had your little performance, now it's my turn. I don't know what the hell's going on here, but I know this much. You didn't kill Mitch, so you can stop pretending you did.

ALIDA: I came stumbling in here, covered with blood!

IAN: Forget it, we're not going to talk about it, we're going to talk about us. You're going to give me some answers, now, finally! Are you reading me?

ALIDA: Give me the wine.

IAN: No.

ALIDA: Give me the wine, Ian.

IAN:	No.
ALIDA:	No wine, no answers.
	IAN hands her the wine.
IAN:	Are you ready now?
ALIDA:	Hit me.
IAN:	You knew Mitch was coming here tonight. You knew it all along. How! How did you know?
ALIDA:	How do you think?
IAN:	You invited him?
ALIDA:	Not exactly.
IAN:	What the hell does that mean!
ALIDA:	Don't shout at me. I'll clam right up if you shout at me.
IAN:	Did you invite him, or didn't you?
ALIDA:	Let's put it this way. I knew he was coming and I knew what he was coming for. All right? But we had a fight, Ian. Over you. He wanted to go too far, so I killed him. You don't believe me, but I did, I really killed him, and I'm not sorry. What did he amount to anyway, what was he? An expert on cruelty—and venereal disease. That's another story. I killed him, and what's more I enjoyed it. That's what marriage does for you, you see? Teaches you what true hatred is!
IAN:	*(Trying to stay calm.)* Why did you let him come here? Alida?
ALIDA:	To save you.
IAN:	From what?
ALIDA:	From me.
IAN:	*(Moves away.)* Oh no you don't, you're not starting that.

ALIDA: I've tried and tried to tell you, but you won't—

IAN: Right, you've got it.

ALIDA: Listen to me, listen! I'd like to be what you think I am—I'd transform myself if I could—but it's not possible. I'm greedy, that's the trouble—a real pig. Restless, too. Not much good to anyone, including myself. And inside my head—here, where it matters—there's a war going on, a trench war. Blood and guts and rats and muck—

IAN: Stop it.

ALIDA: Even in my sleep I can—

            IAN grabs her by the shoulders.

IAN: Alida, just—stop it! Why do you do that to yourself?

ALIDA: You don't believe me. For God's sake, shouldn't I know?

IAN: No! You're the last person who should know. You spend so much time flipping in and out of reality, you don't know what's real anymore. But I do, Alida. I do! Now. I want you to tell me why you let this happen. I want the truth, no matter what it is.

ALIDA: He made me.

IAN: I knew it! I knew he was at the bottom of this. If I ever get my hands on that son-of-a-bitch, I'll kill him.

ALIDA: I've already done that.

IAN: *(Moving, excited.)* So. So! He put you up to this. He made you invite me up here so that he could—what? Scare me off?

ALIDA: Yes.

IAN: Why?

ALIDA: Because he's jealous.

IAN: He still wants you. Or maybe he doesn't really want you but he doesn't want anyone else to have you.

ALIDA: He wants me.

IAN: So. He phones you up—is this how it goes? He phones you up?

ALIDA: What does it matter?

IAN: I need to know this, Alida.

ALIDA: He phones me up.

IAN: Says do me a favour, will you—big favour. Get that boyfriend of yours, that fiancé—did he know I was your fiancé? Never mind. Get him in the car, get him up to the cottage—then clear out for a while, so I can... so I can... *(Beat.)* And you said... *(Faces her.)* What did you say, Alida?

ALIDA: God, you turn me on.

IAN: Alida, I think you should know I'm just about at the end of my—

ALIDA: I wanted to tell you, I really wanted to, I wanted to warn you! That's the truth, Ian. I couldn't.

IAN: Why not?

ALIDA: You don't know him. You don't know what he's capable of.

IAN: You're afraid of him?

ALIDA: Yes! Yes yes yes, don't you understand anything?

IAN: It's more than fear, though, isn't it. It goes a lot deeper than that. He's done a number on you—got you all twisted up. He's got you convinced you're not fit for anyone but him, not for anyone decent. God knows, we've been through that often enough. So naturally...when he makes this phone call you'd obviously... *(Trails off.)* No. It doesn't wash.

ALIDA: He did make me do it. Only not the way you think.

IAN: How?

ALIDA: By knowing me too well. By knowing my worst fears and exploiting them. He doesn't care about anyone but himself and he—knows things about people that are…secret, secret things. He sniffs them out, don't ask me how. He does. Like that time in Peru, we were in Peru I think it was, and there was this river—full of life, teeming, crawly, scaley—and he knew the one thing I could never, ever do was jump in that river, even to put my finger in it meant—pure panic. And so, naturally, that's what I had to do. I had to jump in. He made me, you see? By knowing that I'd rather die than do it. But it wasn't always him. In the same way I've made him do things, go places he was scared of. Oh, yes. Lots of those.

IAN: Such as?

ALIDA: Such as? Oh, you know—suburbia. Shopping malls. Backyards.

IAN: This is another one, isn't it? This is just another goddamn fantasy! Christ, Alida. If you didn't want to marry me, all you had to do was say so.

ALIDA: But I do want to marry you.

IAN: I'd noticed.

ALIDA: (Moves to him.) I can't stand the thought of anyone else having you. (Runs a finger along his spine.) That's the same thing, isn't it?

IAN: I can't believe a word you say, you know that? Do you know what that's like?

ALIDA: Kiss me.

IAN: No.

ALIDA: Please.

IAN: No.

ALIDA: I'll die if you don't. I swear to God, I'll die right here at your feet.

IAN: I wish you would, you know that? I almost wish you
              would.

ALIDA: Please.

IAN: Alida—

ALIDA: Please please please.

IAN: I can't believe the stuff I let you get away with.

              She kisses him seductively; then he holds her off.

              No more lies, Alida.

ALIDA: More.

IAN: No more lies, okay? I want the truth.

ALIDA: I want your mouth.

IAN: Alida—

ALIDA: Gimme, gimme, gimme.

              *She kisses him again. He gives into it for a moment,
              then starts to pull away.*

IAN: No. No. What are you doing? Get away from me. Get
              away from me so I can think! I mean it, Alida.

              She backs away.

              Good. Better. Stay right there.

              *SALOME enters, carrying what looks like a roast on a
              tray; the roast is covered with a tea towel.*

SALOME: *(To ALIDA.)* I've brought you your supper, since
              you're so damned hungry.

ALIDA: Not now, Salome!

SALOME: Yes, now! Are you ready? Are you ready for this?

              *SALOME whips the towel from the tray to reveal
              MITCH's head.*

I didn't think you'd really done it, I thought it was just another lie. How could you really do it?

IAN: My God...

ALIDA moves to SALOME and covers the head with the towel.

ALIDA: Get out of here with that. Now!

She shoves SALOME towards the exit.

SALOME: What am I supposed to do with it?

ALIDA: Bury it. Move!

SALOME exits.

IAN: My God.

ALIDA retrieves the wine, begins to uncork it.

That wasn't real. Was that real?

ALIDA: I think it's time for the truth.

IAN: Oh—boy. I'd better have a look at that. Yeah, definitely. *(Starts off.)*

ALIDA: The truth, Ian.

IAN: Good, great. I'll be right back.

ALIDA: This is a ten second offer.

IAN: *(Stops moving.)* The truth?

ALIDA: In vino veritas. Sit down.

IAN: Was that thing real?

ALIDA: Does it matter?

IAN: Does it matter?!

ALIDA: Sit down, Ian.

He obeys.

                 Are you all right? Going to be sick? You don't feel sorry for him, do you?

IAN: Sorry?

ALIDA: Don't. He's got no one to blame but himself. Now. The truth. What I've orchestrated here tonight is actually a little test.

IAN: A test.

ALIDA: Or you could call it a game, if you wanted to.

IAN: What are you talking about?

ALIDA: I need you, Ian. I needed you before but I'm going to need you a lot more now. You can see for yourself what I've done. I've murdered a man. I've murdered the man who was my husband.

IAN: I'm supposed to go along with this, right? See where it takes us? I mean, this is—pure speculation.

ALIDA: If you like.

IAN: Okay. So—let's see. You'd, uh—you'd want me to lie for you.

ALIDA: I'd want you to lie with me. I like the sound of that.

IAN: You'd want me to lie to the police.

ALIDA: Oh hell no, I can do that for myself. I need someone to replace Mitch. In my life. I need someone with the same inclination. Someone who doesn't give a damn about other people's rules. Someone who is truly free. Because when you're free, Ian, truly free, you are truly alive. *(Moves in.)* You know what I'm talking about. You know the stuff we do. The stuff you like me doing to you.

IAN: Oh God.

ALIDA: And, Ian—listen to me. What we've done so far? That was nothing, that was just a taste. It gets better. It gets higher and higher.

IAN: Oh Jesus.

ALIDA: I know what you're thinking. You're thinking you
                can't push it any higher, but you can. You've got what
                it takes, I know it. I have some experience in these
                things and I can tell. I picked you, Ian. Out of
                thousands. Are you all right?

IAN: No, I'm not all right, are you crazy?! I'm mush, for
                God's sake, I'm—I'm—drowning here.

ALIDA: *(Caresses him.)* Poor Ian.

IAN: Don't do that! Stay away from me, do you
                understand? I'm begging you, Alida. I'm warning
                you.

                ALIDA kisses him, then suddenly pulls back.

ALIDA: You beast. You bit me.

IAN: Did I draw blood.?

ALIDA: No.

IAN: Well, come here, I'll give it another shot.

ALIDA: I need an answer, Ian.

IAN: Tell me you're lying, Alida. You are, aren't you. You
                didn't really kill him.

ALIDA: Are you going to do it, or not?

IAN: Do what exactly?

ALIDA: Whatever we want to do. Whatever we damn well
                decide we want to do.

IAN: Like this, you mean. Like the sort of thing you've
                done tonight?

ALIDA: Maybe.

IAN: Like messing around with people's heads. Like
                murder?

ALIDA: Oh, well. I normally draw the line at that.

IAN: Normally? *(Laughs.)* Good. Good for you, Alida.

ALIDA: Look, Ian., it's a very simple thing. Either it appeals to you, or it doesn't. I know it does.

IAN: No.

ALIDA: Yes.

IAN: No!

ALIDA: Then what are you doing here?

IAN: You know what I'm doing here.

ALIDA: I know why you came. Why did you stay?

            A beat. They face one another.

IAN: Oh no, shit, is that what you think? I don't think that's right. I mean, I guess, at a certain level—a certain intellectual level—

ALIDA: I know what you're feeling. You're shocked at yourself. Don't be. Ian, listen to me. Nobody gets through life without finding a way to get high. Nobody! Look around you. It's a human condition. I'm just a little more honest about it. And a whole lot more original.

            SALOME enters with a garden spade slung across her shoulder.

SALOME: Poor Mitch, poor old Mitch.

ALIDA: *(A warning.)* Salome

SALOME: I don't get it, I just don't get it. I don't know why you had to go and kill him. You just…you went out there and—for Pete's sake, you little whore, you chopped his head off. Like some old rooster.

ALIDA: *(To SALOME.)* You're going to regret this. You know that, don't you?

SALOME: Oh, shit, that's wrong, isn't it. Let's see. (*Adjusts her manner.*) Well, that's done. But if you think I'm burying the rest of him, you can think again.

ALIDA: You're burying the rest of him..

SALOME: No, I'm not! (*Throws down the spade.*) I've been cleaning up your messes half my life. No more. Anyway, what's wrong with him? Why can't he do it? Not dressed for it? I'm surprised he's dressed at all, with you in the vicinity.

ALIDA: I warned you, Salome.

SALOME: I don't give a shit. I'm sick to death of your lousy stinking second-rate games and I'm sick of playing all the bit parts. I keep telling you I need more scope.

ALIDA: (*Moves to her.*) I'll give you scope.

SALOME: Did you tell him about the scars yet? You better do that. Hey, Ian! Here's a good one for you. I'm the one who gave her her scars.

ALIDA: (*To IAN.*) She did! I was seven years old. Seven, and she marked me for life. Bitch. Wicked old bitch.

SALOME: Whore. Lying whore.

IAN: (*An explosion.*) Shut up, both of you! My God, you're depraved, I think you're both depraved! Scars, mutilation, murder? (*Laughs crazily.*) What next? When do you stop, what's it going to take to make you stop?!

SALOME: (*To IAN.*) Have you figured it out yet? Lover?

           ALIDA turns back to SALOME.

ALIDA: Get out of here!

SALOME: Don't worry, I'm going.

           SALOME exits.

IAN: There's no limit to you, is there. There's absolutely nothing you won't say.

ALIDA: She did give me my scars. Listen, I want you to know this. I used to have fainting spells when I was a child. Nobody knew what caused them, just—snap, out like a light. And that Salome, that old witch. While I was out, she'd carve me up. With pinking shears! And when anyone would ask—not that anyone often did, not my loving father, certainly—she'd say I'd done it to myself, was always doing it. The minute she turned her back, snip snip snip. Why would a child do a thing like that, didn't anyone ever want to know?

IAN: (*Sits.*) Enough.

ALIDA: Now, of course, she goes in for other forms of entertainment. She seduces young boys—juicy young boys, firm as peaches, who'd rather die horrible deaths than have sex with her. But she forces herself on them. Oh yes. I've seen it. I've been a witness.

IAN: Alida...you know—know what I'm doing? I'm sitting here—praying—that you're going to walk across to me, and tell me this was all a bad dream, and it's over now, and we can go back to being what we were.

ALIDA: I'm surprised at you. You've been trying for six solid months to find out how I got my scars. Now I tell you, and you act as though you didn't hear.

            IAN suddenly pulls himself to his feet.

IAN: I have to get out of here.

ALIDA: Well, I certainly didn't get them in Florence, I can tell you that. I've never even been there. On the other hand, I have been to Crete. (*Smiles.*)

            IAN casts about in confusion, then begins to gather up his things.

            I take it the answer is no. You're a fool, you know. Where do you think you're going to go? You can't go back where you came from, they won't have you.

You're tainted. You've got an odor about you now, like bad meat. Don't turn your back when I'm talking to you!

IAN: Just let me go, Alida. Okay? While there's still something left of me.

ALIDA: Something left of you! *(Turns away.)* God, what a bore.

IAN: *(Beat.)* Say that again?

ALIDA: You're a bore, a bore, boring.

IAN: Well, this is refreshing. What's this, the truth at last?

ALIDA: I tried, I really tried with you, you know that? Hopeless. And now look at you, just look at you! A big—mopey—baby! What are you moping about, anyway? You're not a child. You knew what you were getting into. And besides—you'll survive. As a matter of *fact*, you'll be better for it. As a matter of fact, you should thank me. I pulled you out of that cement you were imbedded in—the cement you called your life—and I breathed fire into you. You've never been so alive!

IAN: Are you finished?

ALIDA: I'm finished with you.

IAN: That's the best news I've had all night.

He exits.

ALIDA: What a waste. *(Moves after him, calls out.)* Ian! What a waste! Remember I said that.

She stands looking after him for a moment, then moves to the lawn chair, sits, stares off. A few beats. The window swings open and MITCH steps out. He moves quietly in behind her, bends her head back, kisses her.

MITCH: You'll never guess what I've got. *(Draws a mickey from his pocket, runs it around her neck.)* Maybe I'll let you have some, if you're good.

ALIDA: I'm always good.

MITCH: That's why I keep you around.

              He kisses her again, then moves to the table to pour drinks. She stares off.

ALIDA: Look at it, would you? Beautiful. We should get up here more often, you know that? We should really make a point of it. So. Did it work for you?

MITCH: Sure, why not, you?

ALIDA: You don't sound as though you mean that.

              No response. She turns toward him.

              Mitch?

MITCH: Let's have a drink, Alida.

ALIDA: That's no answer.

MITCH: Let's just have a drink, all right?

              MITCH moves back to her, hands her a drink.

ALIDA: What's the matter with you?

MITCH: I'd like to know where Salome is.

ALIDA: You surely don't expect her to show up when she's supposed to.

MITCH: Not after your little performance.

ALIDA: My performance! What about hers?

MITCH: You have to coddle her. If you coddle her, she's fine.

ALIDA: *(Stands.)* Well, I'm sick to death of coddling her. She's finished, Mitch. I expect you to back me up on that.

MITCH: *(Deadly.)* You what. Expect? Is that what you said?

ALIDA: I—she tried to sabotage me.

MITCH: *(Moves in.)* Who do you think you're talking to, here?

SALOME enters.

Save that talk for the bait! *(Turns to SALOME.)* Well?

SALOME: He's gone.

MITCH: Good.

SALOME: I need to talk to you, Mitch.

MITCH: Later.

SALOME: When, later?

MITCH: Tomorrow.

SALOME: This is important to me.

MITCH: *(Faces her.)* Tomorrow.

SALOME: Is that it? That's all you're going to say?

MITCH: Look, Salome—

SALOME: I like to play. I really like to play, you know that. But I won't take orders from her.

ALIDA: Oh, get out of here.

SALOME: *(To ALIDA.)* I'm not talking to you!

MITCH: Okay, both of you—enough.

SALOME: *(To MITCH.)* She kept saying I was drunk. I wasn't drunk.

ALIDA: You certainly were.

SALOME: I was not!

MITCH: Enough. I'm warning you, Salome—

SALOME: Me? What about her?

ALIDA: She's still drunk, I can smell her from here.

SALOME: Lying whore.

MITCH: *(To SALOME.)* Get the fuck out of here! Now!

For a moment SALOME doesn't move. Then she starts off.

We'll talk tomorrow, Salome.

SALOME exits.

Shit.

ALIDA: You have to coddle her. If you coddle her, she's fine.

MITCH: Sloppy! I'm telling you, this has been one fucking sloppy night.

ALIDA: I wouldn't worry about it.

MITCH: You wouldn't, eh. Did you get my keys?

ALIDA: Oh hell.

MITCH: Fuck, Alida, you had your hands all over him.

ALIDA: Well, don't blame me! You're the one who gave them to him.

MITCH: I didn't give them to him, I tossed them to him. You want to know how he caught them? With his tight little ass!

He moves away.

ALIDA: You know what I think? Mitch? I think we should back up and start over again. Concentrate on what really matters. *(Moves in behind him.)* What do you think? We can do that, can't we?

MITCH: Not if I have to kiss you again.

ALIDA starts to move away.

Hey. *(Grabs her.)* You were dynamite tonight.

ALIDA: Was I?

MITCH: TNT.

ALIDA: You weren't so bad yourself. Your assessment?

MITCH: *(Shrugs.)* Not bad.

ALIDA: Not bad?

MITCH: Not stupid, not ugly.

ALIDA: You're teasing me.

MITCH: Am I?

ALIDA: Come on, Mitch. He was intrigued, he really was.

MITCH: Yeah? Well, he's gone, isn't he.

ALIDA: It was a struggle.

MITCH: It was a struggle, all right. You know why? Because you had that poor bastard dancing on so many strings, he couldn't piss unless you pulled one.

ALIDA: *(Beat.)* What the hell is the matter with you?

MITCH: Look, what do you want? Do you want me to tell you he was good? He was good. You did good.

            He salutes her.

ALIDA: Do you mean that?

MITCH: Yeah. I thought he was real—nice.

ALIDA: Nice. What do you mean, nice.

MITCH: It's not a complicated word.

ALIDA: He was not very damn nice and you know it! He was nice, once, when I met him—a nice, decent, boring boy. I changed that. I set him free, set him on fire, showed him what it means to be alive!

MITCH: You're kidding yourself.

ALIDA: I did! And he proved it, tonight. He was with us every inch of the way. Why can't you admit it?

MITCH: Look, you wanted my opinion, you got it.

ALIDA:	Well! If that's the way it is, I think I'll have another drink.
MITCH:	You don't need another drink.
ALIDA:	It's been a long night.
MITCH:	About average.
ALIDA:	It's been one hell of a long night!
MITCH:	Hey, don't take it like this. What did you expect me to say, anyway?
ALIDA:	I expected you to say he was the best.
MITCH:	The best of yours.
ALIDA:	The best of the lot.
MITCH:	No way. Remember Janice?
ALIDA:	No.
MITCH:	Sure you do, you remember Janice.
ALIDA:	How could I? One curvaceous little airhead is pretty much like the rest.
MITCH:	She was no airhead. She had you on your toes. She made you sweat.
ALIDA:	Did she?
MITCH:	Don't give me that—did she. You were sizzling. There was steam rising off the lake, and we weren't even in it. Don't tell me she didn't make you sweat.
ALI DA:	But Ian didn't do that. He didn't make you sweat.
MITCH:	Sweat, fuck. I could hardly stay awake.
ALIDA:	That's why you were so rough on him. Broken whiskey bottles, the works.
MITCH:	Well, what can I say? I was panting for my reward.

He toasts her, drinks, turns away.

ALIDA: You're lying to me. You are. You know you are.

MITCH: *(Beat.)* You jeopardized the game. You jeopardized the whole fucking game, can't you see that?

ALIDA: What are you talking about? You'd better explain yourself.

MITCH: No. *(Moves in on her.)* No, you're the one with the explaining to do. You can start right now. You can start by explaining why it took you so fucking long to get him up here. I mean, I know about your appetite. But six months? And then there's all this fiancé stuff he's laying on me. Fiancé this, fiancé that. And the funny thing is, he's serious. He really thinks he's going to do it, he's practically bought the fucking flowers. Now you explain that to me, Alida. I'm really curious about that!

ALIDA: It was because of his background.

MITCH: His what?

ALIDA: His background, he—comes from this very strict background—he was even engaged to some pallid little church-mouse when I met him—and he had to believe it was leading somewhere, that *we* were, or he couldn't—

MITCH: Perform?

ALIDA: He could perform just fine. But he was feeling guilty and I had to do something.

MITCH: You could have dumped him.

ALIDA: I didn't want to dump him.

MITCH: You broke the rule, Alida. One rule—very simple, very important. No complications! You broke it. I want to know why.

ALIDA: Isn't it obvious? I thought he could do it. I thought he could really do it—if I groomed him well enough.

MITCH: Do what?

ALIDA: There's only one answer to that question.

MITCH: No, Alida. There's two.

            She turns toward him.

ALIDA: Is that what this is all about! It is, isn't it? My God. I
            don't know what to say. So. It's not the game you're
            upset about—there's always another game. It's Ian
            who's upset you. You could see how good he was, a
            real contender—and it scared the hell out of you.

MITCH: I wouldn't go that far.

ALIDA: Come on, Mitch. You were scared to death. Admit it.

MITCH: Fuck, Alida—

ALIDA: I need to hear this.

MITCH: Why?

ALIDA: Because I want you hot and I want you high. And I
            want to know that I did it!

            MITCH grins.

MITCH: Oh, babe. You're something else, you know that? You
            can lie your ass off to any man you meet, you can spin
            out fantasies that run on for weeks. But when I want
            the truth out of you, all I have to do is turn the key.
            Why is that? Huh? Get over here.

ALIDA: Not until you admit it.

MITCH: All right, I was scared. I was fucking scared, all right?
            For maybe three seconds.

ALIDA: You thought I really wanted him.

MITCH: It crossed my mind.

ALIDA: I can't believe it. This is wonderful.

MITCH: Yeah well, don't gloat too much, Alida. You had to
            change the game to do it. It's one thing to come up
            here and have to watch some pimply-faced kid who's

been screwing your ass off prance around like he's the only one who knows how to do it—that's one thing. This fiancé stuff—this six months business—that's something else.

ALIDA: You're the only one I've ever loved. You know that.

MITCH: Are you going to get over here, or what.

ALIDA: *(Moves to him.)* I don't blame you for being scared, though. He was quite a specimen. And you know what? Mitch? He was very good.

MITCH: How good?

ALIDA: As good as I've ever had.

MITCH: Liar. *(Grabs her hair, pulls her head back.)* Liar.

ALIDA: Pants on fire.

MITCH: I'm going to show you what I do to liars.

He kisses her, undoes her robe, moves in tight. Hot stuff. IAN enters, with a rifle. He is very wired. He moves silently in behind MITCH and puts the nose of the rifle against MITCH's neck. MITCH freezes. Then ALIDA freezes.

IAN: Don't stop on my account. I said don't stop!

MITCH tries to turn.

Don't turn.

MITCH freezes again.

It's your rifle and it's loaded. You know it's loaded. Now go ahead—fuck her. Come on! That's what this is all about.

MITCH: No.

IAN: Yes! I've been out there, listening. I've had an earful! Now you fuck her.

MITCH: You're making a mistake.

IAN: Shut up and fuck her!

MITCH: Come here, Alida. Come here!

                ALIDA moves back into MITCH's arms. He kisses her
                woodenly.

IAN: That's right, do it. Come on, do it. Do it! You call that
                doing it?

MITCH: You son of a bitch—

IAN: *(Jams the rifle into his neck.)* I want to see a little steam
                here. I want to see steam rising off the lake. I paid for
                it, Goddamnit. You think that's fun? Man? *(Jabs*
                MITCH with the rifle.) Think that's a picnic? *(Jabs him*
                again.) Man! Now you show me some action. Show
                me how good I was!

ALIDA: Ian, for God's sake—

IAN: *(Swings the rifle on her.)* You are not talking!
                Understand?

MITCH: *(Pulls her into him.)* She understands.

IAN: She better!

MITCH: She does.

IAN: Good. *(To MITCH.)* Now take your clothes off. Take
                your clothes off so you can do it!

                MITCH takes off his jacket.

                That's it. Now your shirt. Your shirt!

                MITCH starts to unbutton his shirt.

                Good. Very good. You're pretty smart, for a dead
                man. *(To ALIDA.)* What are you looking like that for?
                You're not scared, are you? I thought you liked this
                sort of thing. Or maybe you only like it when you get
                to call the shots. Stop looking like that! I'm not going
                to shoot you. *(Laughs crazily.)* Not until you finish,
                anyway.

MITCH takes off his shirt.

(To MITCH.) Good. Now keep going. Keep going!

MITCH pulls one shoe off, then the other. Then he starts on his pants.

This is pretty good. This is going to work out fine, You're going to like this, both of you. It's going to give you a whole new perspective on—on what? Humiliation! Oh, yeah. I think so.

SALOME enters.

SALOME: What's going on here?

IAN swings so that he can keep a line on all three of them.

IAN: Don't move! Don't anybody move!

SALOME: *(To IAN.)* What the hell do you think you're doing?

IAN: Get out of here, Salome!

SALOME: Put that thing down.

IAN: Get out of here or I'll blow you away!

SALOME takes a step towards IAN. He swings to face her. As he does, MITCH suddenly lunges at IAN. IAN turns and fires. MITCH crumples. There's a moment of stunned disbelief; ALIDA drops to her knees next to MITCH.

ALIDA: Mitch?

SALOME runs to MITCH, kneels beside him.

IAN: Oh my God. Oh my God—

ALIDA: Mitch! Answer me. Answer me!

SALOME starts to cry.

SALOME: Oh no. Oh no, Mitch!

IAN: Is this the idea? Hey—hey, Alida! Think I've got the hang of it now? Look at me, God damn you, I want an answer! Is this the kind of high you're after?!

> *No response. IAN tries to get himself in hand, can't do it. He becomes aware of the rifle in his hands and throws it down. He backs away, stares around in confusion, then starts to stumble off. ALIDA gets to her feet.*

ALIDA: Ian? Sweetheart?

> *He stops moving, faces her. She moves toward him.*

> *Blackout.*

> *The End.*

Transit of Venus

This play is dedicated to my father
Victor Horsman,
to my brothers
Doug, Jack, Russ, and Scott,
and to the memory of my brother Gregg

Production Information

Transit of Venus was premiered at the Manitoba Theatre Centre on November 26, 1992 with the following cast:

LE GENTIL .... Jim Mezon
DEMARAIS .... Duncan Ollerenshaw
MARGOT .... Donna Goodhand
CELESTE .... Larissa Lapchinski
MME SYLVIE .... Joyce Campion

Directed by Larry Desrochers
Set and costume design: Doug Paraschuk
Lighting design: Graeme S. Thomson
Stage Manager: Chris Pearce
Assistant Stage Manager: Allan Teichman

Preface

"Sunday the fourth, having awakened at two o'clock in the morning, I heard the sand-bar moaning in the south-east; which made me believe that the breeze was still from this direction... I regarded this as a good omen, because I knew that the wind from the south-east is the broom of the coast and that it always brings serenity; but curiosity having led me to get up a moment afterwards, I saw with the greatest astonishment that the sky was covered everywhere, especially in the north and north-east, where it was brightening; besides there was a profound calm. From that moment on I felt doomed..."

Guillaume Le Gentil de la Galasière
June 1769, Pondichéry, India

This play is based on a true story. There was indeed an astronomer named Guillaume le Gentil de la Galiasière (1725–1792), whose attempts to chart the transits of Venus were foiled by war, weather, circumstance, and bad luck.

Le Gentil's work was part of a major effort by a number of countries to establish the precise distance between the earth and the sun by charting the transits of Venus in 1761 and 1769. This was to be accomplished by a method called triangulation, which required that measurements be taken from widely separated points on the earth's surface. To this end, 120 men were dispatched to 62 separate stations to observe the first transit; 138 men observed the second transit from 63 stations. England, for instance, sent a team to Fort Churchill in Hudson Bay in the fall of 1768 and had it winter over there in order to be on location for the second transit the following June. (The team had requested a "warm and not too out-of-the-way" place.) Another team was sent to Cape Town, where it successfully charted the transit of 1761 but became famous for a very different accomplishment a few years later. The members of this team were Charles Mason and a land surveyor named Jeremiah Dixon. Another well-known transit observer was Captain James Cook who, after helping to chart the transit of 1769 from Tahiti, went on to chart New Zealand and the eastern coastline of Australia.

Most of the details of Le Gentil's life and work during the period reflected in the play are accurate, but I have taken some liberties with history. The real Le Gentil did not return to France between transits. The letter from the British Admiralty which is quoted at the outset of the play was indeed obtained by the French Academy, but for an astronomer other than Le Gentil. Although Le Gentil's studies helped to kindle French interest in the transits, I have probably exaggerated his importance in inspiring international efforts to measure them. Finally, the setting of the play and all the characters other than Le Gentil are fictional, and I have re-imagined the personality and private life of Le Gentil to suit my purposes.

The story of Le Gentil's attempts to chart the transits of Venus is a fascinating one. Most of it could not be included in the play. For those interested in the details the following books will be helpful: *The Transits of Venus: A Study of Eighteenth Century Astronomy* by Harry Woolf; *The Whisper and the Vision: The Voyages of the Astronomers* by Donald Fernie; and *Coming of Age in the Milky Way* by Timothy Ferris. The references to Le Gentil's life and work which appear in the play were drawn from these books, as was the summary of his life which follows.

The Life of Le Gentil

Guillaume le Gentil de la Galasière was destined for the priesthood, but while still a student of theology he happened to hear a lecture by the astronomer Joseph-Nicolas Delisle. He promptly gave up the Church to study astronomy. Before he was 25, he had discovered the Trifid Nebula, a bright diffuse nebula in the constellation Sagittarius. Before he was thirty, he had been awarded a seat in the prestigious Royal Academy of Sciences. He completed important calculations in preparation for the transits of Venus, and was assigned to chart the first transit from Pondichéry in India. In March 1760, at the age of 35, he sailed from France aboard a ship called *Le Berryer*.

Unfortunately, France was at war with England (the Seven Years War). When Le Gentil reached Île de France, now called Mauritius, in July of 1760, Pondichéry was under siege. Because of the war and the vagaries of sea travel, he was not able to get close to Pondichéry until the following May. By then, the colony had fallen. On June 6, 1761, the date of the first transit, Le Gentil was somewhere in the middle of the Indian Ocean. It was a fine, clear day. He was able to watch the transit but couldn't measure it; for that he needed a surface more stable than the heaving deck of a ship at sea.

To salvage something from his voyage, Le Gentil stayed on in the area to do other scientific work. Based at Mauritius, he began a lengthy series of exploratory voyages through the Mascarene Islands, up and down the east coast of Madagascar, and elsewhere in the Indian Ocean. The months slipped into years, and by 1765 he had begun to think of the second transit. Convinced he could obtain more accurate measurements in Manila than elsewhere, he sailed in May 1766 for the Philippines. Hostile conditions there and the preference of the French Academy eventually forced him to leave Manila for Pondichéry, which was once again under French authority. Arriving there in March 1768, he set up his observatory, studied Indian astronomy and waited. Then, early on the morning of June 4, 1769, the date of the second transit, he watched with dismay as an unseasonable storm blew in, obscuring his view of the heavens. (In Manila, the sky was perfectly clear.)

Shortly afterwards, Le Gentil fell ill. It was nearly a year before he was able to leave India for Mauritius, and another year before he was able, after a number of ill-fated attempts, to sail for home. Arriving overland from Spain, he finally set foot again on French soil in October 1771. When he reached his home a few weeks later, he discovered that in his long absence he'd been declared dead, his estate (which had been robbed) was being divided amongst his heirs and creditors, and his seat in the Royal Academy of Sciences had been given away. He was eventually awarded a special seat, but his efforts to regain his estate were long and costly. He gave up active astronomy, married, became a father and wrote his memoirs. He died at the age of sixty-seven.

Acknowledgements

The poem quoted by Celeste in Act One is "On Platonic Love" by Samuel Boyse; it has been edited. Mme. Sylvie's line about destiny in Act One is from *West with the Night* by Beryl Markham. Rousseau's admonition, "No chaste girl has ever read novels," appeared in the preface to his novel *Julie, ou la nouvelle Héloïse*. I couldn't resist using it even though, by most accounts, the novel was not published until 1761. The references to convent life are drawn from *Madame de Sévigné: A Life and Letters* by Frances Mossiker, and from *Les Misérables* by Victor Hugo. The stories about the sea told by Demarais and Le Gentil in Act Two are drawn from *Diaries from the Days of Sail* by R.C. Bell, a compilation of first-hand accounts of life at sea, some of which I have quoted directly or edited slightly. I am also indebted to *Camille: The Life of Camille Claudel* by Reine-Marie Paris. It is Camille's statement, "Of the dream that was my life, this is the nightmare" which Celeste quotes directly in Act Two. Le Gentil's description of Venus in Act One is drawn from several sources, principally *The Encyclopedia Britannica*.

Other books which were especially helpful in writing the play include *Beyond the Reefs* by William Travis; *A Long Desire* by Evan S. Connell; *Starseekers* by Colin Wilson; *Infinite in all Directions* by Freeman Dyson; *The French: Portrait of a People* by Sache de Gramont; *The Enlightenment: An Evaluation of its Assumptions, Attitudes and Values* by Norman Hampson; *The Eighteenth Century in France: Society, Decoration, Furniture* by Pierre Verlet; *A History of Private Life: The Passions of the Renaissance* by Philippe Ariès and Georges Duby, general editors; Roger Chartier, editor and Arthur Goldharnmer, translator; and *A Woman's Life in the Court of the Sun King: Letters of Liselotte von der Pfalz, 1652–1722*, translated and introduced by Elborg Forster.

New France was ceded by France to England under the Treaty of Paris in 1763; it was subsequently renamed Quebec. Celeste refers to Quebec as New France in Act Three because it seemed probable that the original name would still be commonly used in France in 1771.

I would like to thank the Canada Council, the Manitoba Arts Council, Manitoba Theatre Centre and the Manitoba Association of Playwrights for their contribution to the development of this play. I'm grateful to Hans Thater, who first told me about Le Gentil; to the many friends and relatives who offered comments and encouragement, especially Martha Brooks, Stephanie Kostiuk, Mary Valentine and my husband Gary; to George Toles and Svetlana Zylin for their comments on the early drafts; and to Steven Schipper for his ongoing support of my work and his faith in this play. I'm grateful to the actors who gave the play its first reading and to those in the première production, who also participated in a workshop of the play in Toronto in August 1992. In particular, I'm grateful to Larry Desrochers. He became involved in the development of the play after I'd completed the second draft and subsequently spent countless hours discussing, analyzing, and critiquing it. His commitment to *Transit of Venus*, his exacting standards, and his skills as dramaturge, editor, and director helped substantially to shape, focus, and enrich the last two drafts.

Maureen Hunter
November, 1992

Setting

The play takes place in a country home in France in March 1760, July 1766, and November 1771. The windows of this home are outstanding: they soar upwards, dominating the rooms within and opening them to the sun and moon and stars.

The period of the play should be suggested as simply as possible. I like Milan Kundera's words at the outset of his play, *Jacques and his Master*.

"The action takes place in the eighteenth century, but in the eighteenth century as we dream of it today. Just as the language of the play does not aim to reproduce the language of the time, so the setting and costumes must not stress the period. The historicity of the characters... though never in question, should be slightly muted."

The following furniture will be required:
The study: a desk, a few chairs, a telescope;
The sitting room: a settee, a few chairs and small tables;
The observatory: a telescope, a freestanding terrestrial globe, a chair and footstool, a table.

In the original production, the set was designed so that the action could flow freely through the study and sitting room, up a set of curved stairs to the observatory. Since space in the observatory was limited and more distant from the audience, opportunities were taken at appropriate moments in both Act One, scene four, and Act Two, scene three, to move the action down the stairs into the study or sitting room.

Characters
(ages apply to the year 1760)

Act One

Scene One

> *The study. 5:00 a. m. Heavy rain. There's a commotion offstage, then LE GENTIL strides on. His outer clothes—coat, hat, gloves, boots—are mud-spattered and drenched from the rain. He carries a lantern and a leather saddle bag. He moves to the desk, sets down the lantern, tosses the saddlebag across a chair, peels off his gloves, throws them down and shouts.*

LE GENTIL: Demarais! *(Pulling off his overcoat.)* Demarais! Get up and get in here. Now.

> *He tosses his overcoat across a chair, lights a candle, opens a drawer, and takes out a carafe and glasses. DEMARAIS runs on.*

DEMARAIS: Well?

LE GENTIL: I've ridden all night straight into a driving rain and all you can say is "Well"?

DEMARAIS: We've got a ship.

LE GENTIL: That's more like it.

DEMARAIS: We've got a ship!

LE GENTIL: We've got a ship, Demarais.

> *DEAMRAIS lets out a whoop.*

She's called *Le Berryer* and she sails on the twenty-sixth.

DEMARAIS: From?

LE GENTIL: Brest. She's a troop ship but she'll get us there all right.

              He pours drinks.

DEMARAIS: How soon do we leave?

LE GENTIL: As soon as we're packed. The roads are treacherous, it will be slow going all the way to the sea. Well, what are you waiting for? Get over here and have a drink with me. If this isn't a night for celebration, there will never be one in our lifetime.

              DEMARAIS joins LE GENTIL. They raise their glasses.

              To India! May her skies be clear.

DEMARAIS: To India, and the ship that takes us there!

              They drink.

LE GENTIL: You're grinning like a maniac.

DEMARAIS: No more than you.

LE GENTIL: I am a maniac. Haven't I ridden six hours through the rain? I'm soaked to the bone, but what a ride, Demarais, what a night.

DEMARAIS: It can't be true. I must be dreaming.

LE GENTIL: It's no dream, I promise you that.

DEMARAIS: A troop ship?

LE GENTIL: A troop ship.

DEMARAIS: I suppose that means we're liable to see action.

LE GENTIL: Oh, that's been taken care of.

DEMARAIS: What do you mean?

LE GENTIL: I mean that in my pocket, right here over my heart, lies a letter telling any damned Englishman we run into to back off and let us through.

DEMARAIS: How did you get it?

LE GENTIL: Delisle got it.

DEMARAIS: How?

LE GENTIL: He wrote the British Admiralty. And damned if they didn't answer! Here, you know English, read it for yourself.

DEMARAIS: *(Taking the letter, he reads.)* "To the captains and commanders of His Majesty's ships and vessels: Whereas the Academy of Sciences at Paris has appointed several of its members to proceed to different parts of the world to observe the transit of Venus over the sun, one of whom, the bearer, Monsieur Le Gentil de la Galasière, is to make such observation from India, and whereas—

LE GENTIL: My God, the way they talk.

DEMARAIS: "The said Monsieur de la Galasière must not meet with any interruption in his travels, you are hereby most strictly required and directed—" *(He breaks off.)* This is incredible! *(Resumes reading.)* "—not to molest his person or effects—" *(Breaks off.)* That includes me, I take it. *(Resumes.)* "—upon any account, but to suffer him to proceed without delay in the execution of his design." *(Folding the letter.)* Remarkable.

LE GENTIL: It is remarkable. Unfortunately, it has its limitations.

DEMARAIS: Such as?

LE GENTIL: If we do run into the English, they'll come at us, cannons blazing, and the reading of any documents will be strictly an afterthought. But we won't tell the women that. *(Refills the glasses.)* How are they?

DEMARAIS: The women? Fine.

LE GENTIL: All of them?

DEMARAIS: All of them.

LE GENTIL: Even the little stubborn one who leads us by the nose?

DEMARAIS: Even her.

LE GENTIL: Good.

              They raise their glasses.

              To Venus, and the secrets she will share with us.

DEMARAIS: To Venus!

              They drink.

LE GENTIL: Now. You go and finish dressing; I'll find some clothes that are clean and dry. Then we'll set to work. We have a lot to do, and very little time.

              DEMARAIS starts off.

              Demarais? Don't wake anyone. The longer we keep the women in the dark, the more we'll accomplish.

              DEMARAIS exits. LE GENTIL exits.

Scene Two

              The sitting room. 9:00 a.m. Overcast. MARGOT sits sewing. CELESTE enters.

MARGOT: There you are, Celeste! No kiss for your mother this morning?

              CELESTE moves to MARGOT and kisses her.

              Sit down, dear, quickly. I've set out some work for you there. Celeste?

              CELESTE sits.

              Pick it up, please, and get started. We can't have you sitting here empty-handed when she comes in. Bad enough you should be late—

CELESTE: A minute or two.

MARGOT: Please pick it up, Celeste.

CELESTE obeys.

You look pale. You didn't sleep?

CELESTE: On the contrary.

MARGOT: You don't look as though you have. You've lost all the colour you had when you came home. I wish you'd let me mix you up one of my special remedies. Three sips will cure you of anything!

CELESTE throws down her sewing in frustration.

I'm only trying to make you smile.

CELESTE: I loathe mending.

MARGOT: Perhaps you'd prefer to darn. There's a bundle of socks there

CELESTE: I loathe darning, too.

MARGOT: You seem to loathe everything, these days, that smacks of work.

CELESTE: Only if it requires a needle.

MARGOT: You can't live in this house and not contribute, Celeste. Not under any circumstances. Even Madame Sylvie contributes, in her own way. As a matter of fact, considering her position—

CELESTE: He's back, you know.

MARGOT: *(Beat.)* I know.

CELESTE: Have you seen him?

MARGOT: No.

CELESTE: Has Madame Sylvie?

MARGOT: I've no idea.

CELESTE: If he's seen her before seeing me—

MARGOT: Celeste!

CELESTE turns away.

I can't imagine what makes you think he's under any obligation—

CELESTE: Did he send down for breakfast?

MARGOT: If I tell you, will you set to work?

CELESTE: Did he!

MARGOT: Yes.

CELESTE: One breakfast, or two?

MARGOT: Two. One for him and one for Demarais. Now that's it, Celeste, that's all I know.

CELESTE: So! They're holed up in there, the two of them. Doing what, I wonder. Plotting how to keep us in the dark!

MARGOT: Oh, I doubt that. I doubt very much if we're on their minds at all.

CELESTE gives MARGOT a contemptuous glance.

Why do you look at me like that?

CELESTE falters, and quickly picks up her work.

I know how you feel about him, Celeste. But you can't expect him to feel the same about you.

CELESTE: Mother, just don't talk about it. Please! You know I can't bear it.

MARGOT: Celeste, for pity's sake—

CELESTE: Please!

She concentrates fiercely on her work.

MARGOT: We can't go on like this forever, you know. We can't keep dancing around the subject. Sooner or later, difficult as it is, we shall have to discuss it. Are you afraid that I'll be critical of you? But how can I be? How can I criticize you for having feelings that I myself—have had? I know exactly how you feel about him, and it's because I know that I think I can—

CELESTE stands abruptly. MARGOT catches her hand.

I want to help you. Can't you see that? How am I to help you if you won't—

CELESTE runs toward the exit. MARGOT stands.

Celeste!

MME SYLVIE enters, nearly colliding with CELESTE.

MME SYLVIE: Celeste.

CELESTE tries to move past but MME SYLVIE puts out a hand and stops her.

How are you this morning, my dear?

CELESTE: Fine.

MME SYLVIE: You say that as though you'd bitten the word from a bulb of garlic. Where are you off to, in such a hurry?

CELESTE shrugs.

Then perhaps you'll stay. I could do with a little of your impertinence this morning. It always brightens my outlook.

MARGOT: Don't encourage her, please.

MME SYLVIE: *(To CELESTE.)* Will you?

MARGOT: Of course she'll stay. She'll be happy to. *(She sits.)* Come and sit down, Celeste.

CELESTE sits. MME SYLVIE turns to the windows.

MME SYLVIE: Look at it, would you? If it would only rain again, instead of hanging there. I have no stomach for this kind of weather, it's so…

MARGOT: Dreary.

MME SYLVIE: I was going to say so English. *(She sits.)* Well, what do
                we have this morning, mending? Oh, joy.

                She takes up some mending.

MARGOT: There's no need for you to do that, Madame, if you'd
                rather not, now that Celeste is here. They did teach
                her something at the convent, you know. She sews
                quite a fine seam, when she puts her mind to it. And
                she's anxious to keep her hand in.

MME SYLVIE: Are you, Celeste?

CELESTE: If you want to know the truth, I—

MARGOT: Spare us the truth, Celeste, would you…on such an
                English day?

                CELESTE takes up her work. Silence.

MME SYLVIE: When I was at the convent—of course, that was long
                ago, almost in the last century—they didn't teach us
                much of anything. A little Catechism. How to scrawl
                a letter of condolence. How to raise one's voice in
                song—preferably religious. How to enter a salon
                gracefully, and leave it tactfully. That was about it. I
                spent more time being punished than I ever spent at
                learning. I remember having to make the sign of the
                cross on the chapel floor, by licking the stones with
                my tongue. That was for breaking the silence. And if
                I grimaced, I had to do it again—for wincing in the
                face of the Lord. *(Laughs.)* Well, I did a lot of wincing,
                I can tell you. That's what saved me.

CELESTE: Saved you, Madame?

MME SYLVIE: From the convent. I was deemed unfit for God, and
                sent home. My sisters were not so fortunate. There's a
                lesson in that, which I assure you I have not forgotten.
                (Beat.) I'm surprised at you, Margot. You're not going
                to let that pass?

MARGOT: Let—what pass, Madame?

MME SYLVIE: Ah.

> *MME SYLVIE glances from MARG0T to CELESTE.*

I suppose you know my son is back.

CELESTE: Have you seen him?

MME SYLVIE: He rode all night from Paris, if you can imagine, through that rain. Offered himself up as an open invitation to thieves. Risked his neck, his health, and his horse... the roads, I understand, are dreadful.

CELESTE: But have you seen him?

MME SYLVIE: No, Celeste, I haven't. I imagine he'll come looking for us in his own good time.

CELESTE: I don't see why we should have to sit and wait until it suits him to see us.

MARGOT: Celeste!

CELESTE: Well, after all, there are three of us and only one of him.

MARGOT: Forgive her, Madame, she—

MME SYLVIE: *(Overlapping.)* She has a point. I confess to feeling a little annoyed with him myself. Not only annoyed, but curious. What do you suppose has happened?

CELESTE: I think he's got a ship.

> *For a moment, everything stops.*

MARGOT: Surely not. Where would he get a ship in wartime? *(To MME SYLVIE.)* That would be next to impossible.

CELESTE: Not for him.

MARGOT: Even for him. That's a wild guess, nothing more. She has no way of knowing, Madame.

CELESTE: He's got a ship, I can feel it.

MARGOT: Celeste, please! This is the last thing Madame wants to hear.

MME SYLVIE: *(Standing.)* Never mind, Margot. There's enough trouble in the world this morning, don't you think, without our squabbling?

> *She moves to a window, opens it, and breathes deeply.*

What is it today, the tenth? And March, of course. In my entire life, I don't believe that any good thing ever came to me in March.

CELESTE: I'm sorry, Madame. I shouldn't have said it.

MME SYLVIE: On the contrary, Celeste, you've done me a service. You've prepared me for a possibility I'd convinced myself I needn't consider. I was so certain that with the war—

MARGOT: That's what we all thought, Madame.

MME SYLVIE: But you see, I should have known. Once he'd made up his mind, he'd hardly let a little thing like a war stop him.

CELESTE: What will you do, Madame? Will you send for him?

MME SYLVIE: Send for him? Oh no, I think not. Patience gets the better of the buttermilk. You've heard that expression, I think?

CELESTE: *(Standing abruptly.)* Well, I'm sorry, I can't do it. I can't sit here waiting patiently for the privilege of hearing his announcement.

> *She starts off.*

MARGOT: Celeste—

MME SYLVIE: You'd better stay, Celeste, he's sure to—

CELESTE: Bugger him.

> *CELESTE exits. They stare after her, stunned. Then MME SYLVIE draws the window shut.*

MME SYLVIE: This has become a very complicated household.

MARGOT: I'm so sorry, Madame.

MME SYLVIE: Margot, Margot, you must stop apologizing. It's become quite tedious. Oh God. Now I've hurt your feelings.

MARGOT: No.

MME SYLVIE: I have.

MARGOT: I feel as though I'm losing her, Madame. As though I'm reaching for her across a yawning chasm. In my dreams I see her fall! *(With difficulty.)* I seem to have set a very bad example—

MME SYLVIE: Nonsense. You've been with us now ten years. A better housekeeper, a better companion I have never had. But you have one fault. You want none of the credit when things go well, and all of it when things go wrong. That's not fair of you. We're bound up in this, every one of us, like barrels lashed together and thrown into the sea. *(Sits.)* Come, why so pensive?

MARGOT: I was just trying to imagine where a fifteen-year-old girl would learn a word like that.

MME SYLVIE: Like what, like "bugger"? Not from the nuns.

Suddenly, LE GENTIL enters.

LE GENTIL: Hello, Mother.

MME SYLVIE: Guillaume!

LE GENTIL: *(Kissing her cheek.)* How are you?

MME SYLVIE: Nearly dead, I think.

LE GENTIL: You always say that when I've been away.

MME SYLVIE: Well, one of these days it will be true.

He kisses her again, then turns to MARGOT.

LE GENTIL: Margot.

MARGOT: Monsieur.

LE GENTIL: You're well, I hope?

MARGOT: Very well.

LE GENTIL: Good.

He begins to move restlessly around the room.

MARGOT: You'll want coffee, Madame. I'll see to it myself, I
                 think.

She stands, and starts off.

MME SYLVIE: Margot? With a little honey, so as not to burn the
                 chest.

MARGOT: Of course.

MARGOT exits.

MME SYLVIE: You'll join me, won't you, Guillaume? Oh, don't look
                 so worried. I promise not to pester you with
                 questions about Paris. Or the weather, or the roads.
                 (Taking up her work.) Or how well you slept last night.

LE GENTIL: I slept very well.

MME SYLVIE: On horseback?

LE GENTIL: *(Laughs.)* I never manage to get anything past you, do
                 I? *(He leans close, inspecting her work.)* What are you
                 working on there, an altar cloth?

MME SYLVIE: Wouldn't you be surprised if I were.

He laughs again and moves away. She watches him.

                 You always seem so restless, whenever you're in this
                 room. Why is that?

LE GENTIL: Mother, there's something I have to tell you.

MME SYLVIE: You've got a ship.

LE GENTIL: Thank you.

MME SYLVIE: I hope you realize you owe it all to me. I prayed you
                 wouldn't get one—which of course, considering my
                 unique relationship with God, virtually ensured that
                 you would.

LE GENTIL: It's a troop ship, actually, so we won't be without protection.

MME SYLVIE: Ah.

LE GENTIL: And if we should run into trouble, I'll be carrying a letter from the first Lord of the British Admiralty, which guarantees us safe passage.

MME SYLVIE: Really! How impressive. Will they read it after they attack, do you think? Or before.

LE GENTIL: *(Sitting next to her.)* Try to be happy for me, Mother. This is what I've worked towards, since the day I discovered astronomy.

MME SYLVIE: You mean since the day you discovered that the title of savant sat more comfortably on your shoulders than the robes of a priest.

               LE GENTIL turns away; she takes his hand.

               Forgive me. I never wanted the Church to have you; I never felt the Church deserved you.

LE GENTIL: On the contrary, I never deserved the Church.

MME SYLVIE: Well, you see what a heretic I am. You leave immediately?

LE GENTIL: Tomorrow morning.

MME SYLVIE: How are the roads?

LE GENTIL: As smooth as the floor of this room.

MME SYLVIE: Liar. But look at me, fretting about the roads. The roads are now the least of my concerns.

LE GENTIL: I'm going to be fine, Mother. I have no doubt about that. In three years' time, we'll be sitting here together—you and I and Celeste—with all my adventures behind us, and no need to be separated again. Where is she, by the way? I thought she might be here with you.

MME SYLVIE: She was; she left. I don't know where she's gone but I'd relish telling you what her parting words were.

LE GENTIL: I'd better see her.

He prepares to stand.

MME SYLVIE: Guillaume. Spare me a minute or two. Your little Celeste is much younger than I am, she can wait. As a matter of fact, a little waiting might improve her. Will you stay?

LE GENTIL: *(Playfully.)* Only if you promise not to wear me down with tears.

MME SYLVIE: If I thought it would keep you here, I'd shed an ocean of tears. I know better. Now listen. I know how much it means to you, to be able to make this trip. I do know that, in spite of the way I behave. I know you've waited a very long time—

LE GENTIL: Seven years.

MME SYLVIE: And that for you it's both an opportunity and an adventure.

LE GENTIL: And an obligation, Mother. I owe it to the Academy, and to France. After all—

MME SYLVIE: *(Drily.)* Yes, yes, I know all about these obligations. What concerns me is the mess you're leaving behind. You've sown havoc in this household; that's the fact of the matter. And now, when you're most needed, you're going to slip away on us. For years!

He stands and moves away.

LE GENTIL: It's all become a little awkward.

MME SYLVIE: It certainly has.

LE GENTIL: It will sort itself out, while I'm gone.

MME SYLVIE: That's just the point; it won't sort itself out. It's up to you to do that—now, before you leave.

LE GENTIL: What would you like me to do?

MME SYLVIE: I'd like you to clarify your intentions.

LE GENTIL: Surely my intentions are obvious.

MME SYLVIE: To whom?

LE GENTIL: To everyone!

MME SYLVIE: *(With a sigh.)* Guillaume, you're thirty-five years old. You've had a great many women in your life—

LE GENTIL: That's right, I have.

MME SYLVIE: I don't say that out of pride.

LE GENTIL: Or out of shame, I hope.

MME SYLVIE: *(Letting this pass.)* All I'm saying is, at a certain point you lose credibility.

LE GENTIL: With whom?

MME SYLVIE: With women! Come, you're not going to make me lead you through this. You know what I'm talking about. No one seems to know what to believe. The one you say you love doubts you, the one you turn your back on dares to hope—

LE GENTIL: Margot has no business to hope. That sounds callous, but it's true. I never pretended our relationship was anything but what it was.

MME SYLVIE: A convenience? I'm sorry, but you see that's just my point. Look at the uncertainty you've created. Uncertainty, antagonism, despair: the house is awash in it.

LE GENTIL: If I'd known I was going to fall in love with Celeste, I'd have stayed well away from her mother, believe me. Well away! How was I to know? Little Celeste! In my mind she was always five years old.

MME SYLVIE: I'm not asking you to defend your behaviour, I'm asking you to address the problem you've created. I have to live in this house while you're away. I'd prefer that it didn't function like an armed camp.

LE GENTIL: Yes, all right, whatever you like.

MME SYLVIE: It's Margot in particular that I—

LE GENTIL: I'll speak to her.

MME SYLVIE: It's not my place, you see? And it's very awkward for me, knowing what I know—

LE GENTIL: I understand. I'm sorry. There's some part of me, it seems, that's never managed to believe it. Every morning when I wake, for a second or two I'm confused: is it a dream, or has it really happened? It wasn't supposed to happen, I can tell you that; it wasn't in my plans at all. I didn't think I'd ever want to marry, or if I did it would be late in life, when there was nothing left to do. But I look at Celeste, and my knees shake like a school-boy's. Celeste! I'll never understand it. One day she was a child, and the next... And when I think how easily I might have missed her! If I'd left six months ago, as I had hoped to, or if she had stayed away a few months more, everything would have been different. Everything! I'd have sailed away without a backward glance. *(Turning to MME SYLVIE.)* Tell me, Mother, do you believe in destiny?

MME SYLVIE: Not at all. Though I have noticed that it seems to get up early in the morning, and go to bed very late at night.

LE GENTIL: *(Laughs.)* That's very clever.

MME SYLVIE: It's not original.

LE GENTIL: *(Sitting.)* You approve of my choice, don't you, Mother?

MME SYLVIE: I think it will shock a sufficient number of the right people.

LE GENTIL: Seriously.

MME SYLVIE: I like Celeste very much. I particularly like her spirit. I'd hate to see it broken.

LE GENTIL: I have no intention of breaking it. On the contrary, I'm doing what's best for both of us. By the time I get back, she'll be eighteen—a much more suitable age.

MME SYLVIE: What if you lose her?

LE GENTIL: I won't.

MME SYLVIE: Always so certain!

LE GENTIL: I won't lose her.

MME SYLVIE: What if you're wrong?

He hesitates.

LE GENTIL: If I'm wrong, my soul will wither up and die. And that will be the end of Le Gentil. And if you ever tell her I said that, I'll deny it.

MME SYLVIE: Why?

LE GENTIL: She has an instinct for the master stroke—just as I do, I suppose. Fortunately, I've had a little more experience.

LE GENTIL kisses her and stands.

MME SYLVIE: My heart goes with you, all the way to India.

LE GENTIL: I'll miss you, Mother. Pray for me.

MME SYLVIE: Oh, you don't want my prayers. There's no telling what my prayers might do. Drive you straight into the arms of the English!

LE GENTIL: I'm not worried about the English. You know as well as I do: with all our faults, God loves the French the best.

LE GENTIL exits.

Scene Three

> *The study; immediately following. DEMARAIS enters, carrying a chest. He sets it down, begins packing instruments, books, etc. CELESTE runs on. An awkward pause.*

CELESTE: So! I was right. He has got a ship.

DEMARAIS: *(Resuming packing.)* Finally.

CELESTE: Well, good for him! And good for you, Demarais. And as for me, well, I'm sure he would have told me, sometime before the turn of the century,

> *DEMARAIS deems it wiser not to comment.*

When do you leave?

DEMARAIS: Tomorrow.

> *The word hits CELESTE like a blow.*

CELESTE: So soon!

DEMARAIS: It may be soon to you but I, for one, had begun to think the day would never come.

CELESTE: It's all decided, then?

DEMARAIS: Oh yes. *(With a certain satisfaction.)* There'll be no stopping him now.

CELESTE: What is it called, this place he's going to?

DEMARAIS: Pondichéry.

CELESTE: Pondichéry! Even the sound of it is strange. I can't imagine it. I don't even know where it is!

DEMARAIS: It's a long way from France, I can promise you that.

CELESTE: Are you afraid, Demarais?

DEMARAIS: A little.

CELESTE: What of?

DENIARAIS: Of missing France.

CELESTE: Is that all? I would have thought you'd say the English, since we seem to be at war with them. They eat their children, don't they? And scorn the Blessed Virgin. That sounds quite frightening to me. And what about the sea, and sickness? Hurricanes!

DEMARAIS: I'm afraid of all those things. Is that what you want to hear? I don't mind admitting it. But I'd rather die than stay behind.

CELESTE: He's not, though, is he. He's not afraid of anything.

DEMARAIS: You'd have to ask him about that.

CELESTE: I'm asking you.

DEMARAIS: Probably not.

CELESTE: *(Beat.)* You don't approve of me, do you, Demarais?

               DEAMRAIS picks up a book. She takes it.

               Come, we won't be seeing each other for a long, long time. Why not be honest?

DEMARAIS: It has nothing to do with me, one way or the other.

               CELESTE knocks the lid of the chest with one hand; it slams shut.

               I don't think you should have tried to stop him.

CELESTE: Is that what I did?

DEMARAIS: Well, you've made it awfully difficult for him to leave. You don't seem to appreciate what's at stake here. You act as though the entire enterprise were trivial, when the truth is it's unique in the history of science. There are teams going out from half a dozen countries to more than sixty sites. Cape Town, Rodrique, Siberia—

CELESTE: Have I really made it difficult for him?

               DEMARAIS throws the chest lid open.

	Well, he's going, isn't he!
DEMARAIS:	Thank God.
CELESTE:	So I don't see that it was ever very difficult.

She tosses the book in the chest and moves away.

DEMARAIS: I don't know what it is you're after. You asked me a question, I answered it. Because of you, he actually considered not going to India—

CELESTE: Actually considered!

DEMARAIS: He's a great man, Celeste; a great scientist. Why does that make you angry? It should make you proud. He discovered the Trifid Nebula when he was twenty-four. At twenty-eight, he had a seat in the Academy. He's done more calculations on the transit of Venus than anyone in France, possibly anyone in the world. It's because of his calculations that all these teams are going out. How could you expect him to stay behind? His name, Celeste, is going down in history; I predict it. Because once this transit is over and the measurements are in, we'll be able, finally and conclusively, to calculate the distance from the earth to the sun. Think of it! The final problem of astronomy will be solved.

CELESTE: Demarais? Have you ever been in love?

DEMARAIS: *(Resuming packing.)* No, and from what I've observed I'm inclined to hope I never am.

CELESTE: I can't remember a time when I wasn't in love. When I was five years old, and my mother first came to work here, I used to creep into this room, sometimes, or into his observatory, and watch him while he worked. He never knew I was there, I was always very careful not to make a sound. He was so certain in his movements, so swift and definite. He seemed so strong. Then later, all the years I was away, I'd often lie in bed at night, thinking of him. I'd picture him peering up into the sky through his telescope, and I'd imagine that instead of the moon or some cold star up there, it was me he saw, my face. You see? Even as a child, I wanted... I wanted him to be as intrigued with me as he was with his damned stars.

DEMARAIS: Well then, you should be happy. You got what you wanted.

CELESTE: But not the way I wanted it! I keep feeling that I've done something wrong. It's because of my mother, I think. We shouldn't take our happiness at the price of someone else's pain. That kind of happiness is tainted. Isn't it? God would never condone it. Would he?

DEMARAIS: Well, I don't know much about God—

CELESTE: No.

DEMARAIS: But if you're worried about this, you know where to go.

CELESTE: Where?

DEMARAIS: To a priest.

CELESTE: He's my priest.

DEMARAIS: *(Genuinely shocked.)* Celeste!

CELESTE: It's the truth.

DEMARAIS: Then go to him.

LE GENTIL enters, with a letter.

LE GENTIL: I want you to do something for me, Demarais. I've prepared a list of instructions—*(Breaking off.)* Celeste!

CELESTE moves swiftly towards the exit.

Just a minute, I want to talk to you.

CELESTE exits.

Celeste! *(He turns back.)* Damn. *(Throwing the letter on the desk.)* She knows now, I suppose?

DEMARAIS gestures towards the chest.

Well, I'm not going to chase after her, that's certain. A little waiting may improve her, don't you think?

MARGOT enters.

MARGOT: You wanted to see me?

LE GENTIL: Yes. *(To DEMARAIS.)* That's a list of instructions, for my solicitor. I want you to take it to him. Do it now, Demarais.

DEMARAIS takes the letter and exits. LE GENTIL sits at the desk; he glances through a ledger. He avoids meeting MARGOT's eyes.

You got my list?

MARGOT: Just now.

LE GENTIL: You'll manage all right?

MARGOT: There's a great deal to do, and very little time—

LE GENTIL makes an impatient gesture.

We'll manage. It's going to be a long three years, Guillaume.

LE GENTIL: Listen, Margot, there's something I have to say to you. I should have said it weeks ago, but I thought— *(He breaks off, turns away.)* Well. Something unforeseen has happened, something rather strange, I'm…

MARGOT: It must be strange indeed. I don't believe I've ever seen you at a loss for words.

LE GENTIL: I'm in love with your daughter and I intend to marry her when I return. With your blessing, I hope. There, that's it, that's all of it.

A very awkward silence.

You expected this, I think.

MARGOT: No.

LE GENTIL: I thought Celeste might have—

MARGOT: Not at all.

LE GENTIL: Or that you would assume—

MARGOT: Assume? What was I to assume? Clearly, she's infatuated with you, but I'm hardly in a position to condemn her for that. And as for you, well. It didn't occur to me—*(She breaks off; beat.)* Have you told her? Yes, of course you have. She knows perfectly well that you intend to marry her. And Madame, your mother, she knows as well?

LE GENTIL: Yes.

MARGOT: Everyone knows! Everyone's known all along, apparently. Except me.

            He begins to move irritably around the room.

            But now you've told me. Now, on the eve of your departure. Why? If it wasn't necessary to tell me before—

LE GENTIL: It seemed important to clarify things.

NIARGOT: Important to whom? Celeste?

LE GENTIL: To Mother.

MARGOT: Ah! She put you up to it.

LE GENTIL: She asked me to speak to you, yes.

MARGOT: Otherwise you wouldn't have bothered.

LE GENTIL: Definitely not. Better a hurricane at sea, than this!

MARGOT: *(With a little laugh.)* Poor Guillaume. I suppose I am behaving badly. Like a wife, in fact. When in reality it seems my role is to be that of mother-inlaw.

            Instinctively, he moves to touch her.

            Don't.

LE GENTIL: Please, I—

MARGOT: Don't touch me.

LE GENTIL: For God's sake, Margot, you had to know!

MARGOT: How? How could I possibly know, when no one would speak to me? Every time your name comes up, she flies out of the room. Every time I look at you, you turn away.

LE GENTIL: You could have asked. You could have come to me at any time—

MARGOT: As you could have come to me.

LE GENTIL: *(Turning away.)* I was negligent, obviously.

MARGOT: I was blind!

LE GENTIL: *(Beat.)* I swear to you, Margot, on everything that's holy: this is the last thing I ever would have dreamt I'd have to tell you.

                 He moves to the windows and stands with his back to her.

MARGOT: You haven't touched her. Have you?

LE GENTIL: Margot—

MARGOT: No, of course you haven't. Another man—one of those mincing, scented courtiers you so enjoy mocking—a man like that wouldn't hesitate. Out of the mother's bed, into the daughter's! For you, of course, that would be out of the question. No doubt that makes her even more appealing.

LE GENTIL: What are you saying?

MARGOT: Oh, Guillaume, I know you so well. It's not the aim that intrigues you, it's the quest. And it's a meager quest indeed without an obstacle.

LE GENTIL: Listen to me. There are several reasons why I haven't touched Celeste, one of which is my respect for you.

But to suggest that somehow makes her more appealing—

MARGOT: Doesn't it?

He moves abruptly downstage.

LE GENTIL: I refuse to go on with this conversation. I've had enough women in my life, I assure you, to know when I've found one worth waiting for!

MARGOT: This is my daughter we're talking about. This is my Celeste, my jewel! You want me to believe that you love her. How can I? How can I believe that a man in your position, with your experience could fall head over heels in love with a—*(She breaks off.)* My God, Guillaume. She's so young!

LE GENTIL: I'm aware of that, believe me. That's why I think it's just as well I'm going away. By the time I get back—

MARGOT: So young, and so impetuous.

LE GENTIL: She's a little impetuous—

MARGOT: Very.

LE GENTIL: Yes, all right, she's very young and very impetuous. That doesn't change anything.

MARGOT: I won't have her tossed aside, not my Celeste. She's—

LE GENTIL: Enough! Enough of this. I'm not a weather vane, spinning in the wind. I've told you my intentions; now you can plan around them. Do you understand?

MARGOT: Perfectly.

LE GENTIL: Good.

Realizing she's been dismissed, MARGOT turns to leave.

Margot, I—realize our relationship, the one we had—ended badly. But I wouldn't want to leave here tomorrow knowing you felt that I'd misled you in some way. I didn't do that, did I?

MARGOT: No.

LE GENTIL: You're sure?

MARGOT: Quite.

LE GENTIL: Good. Thank God for that. I have your blessing, then?

MARGOT: Pardon me?

LE GENTIL: On this marriage.

MARGOT: *(Beat.)* What have I ever denied you?

> *She exits. He stares after her, briefly, then moves to the stairs leading to the observatory and climbs them, two at a time. As he does so, the light begins to change.*

Scene Four

> *The observatory and the stairs leading up to it. The next day, 4:00 a.m. Moonlight spills through the windows. LE GENTIL stands staring at the sky. He is fully dressed but instead of a jacket there's a robe across his shoulders. CELESTE appears at the foot of the stairs, wearing a nightgown and carrying a candle. She stares up towards the observatory, hesitates, gathers her courage, and climbs the stairs. She enters the room quietly and stands motionless, staring at LE GENTIL, who senses her presence and turns. He stares at her for a long moment, then lets out a breath.*

LE GENTIL: Well, look at you. Look at me! And they say that God has no sense of humour.

CELESTE: I don't—

LE GENTIL: Understand? I think you do. *(He moves downstage.)* Come and sit down.

CELESTE: I only came to—

LE GENTIL: I know why you came. *(He points to a chair.)* Sit.

> *She obeys.*

I was thinking of coming to you, just now. I was thinking I'd try and find you, wherever it is you sleep. It just occurred to me that I don't know—where you sleep, or how. I don't know a lot of things I really ought to know. I've taken too much for granted.

CELESTE: All you have to do is ask.

LE GENTIL: But I don't always get what I ask for. Do I, Celeste?

CELESTE: What do you mean?

LE GENTIL: I sent for you today. Three times. Three times you didn't come.

CELESTE: I know. I'm sorry, I was sulking.

LE GENTIL: Why?

CELESTE: Why not? I do it pretty well.

LE GENTIL: You were sulking because I'm going away.

CELESTE: No, not because of that.

LE GENTIL: Because...

CELESTE: Because I want to be the one you come to first. Why shouldn't I be? Why must I always get things second hand?

LE GENTIL: You wouldn't get them second hand if you would come when you are sent for.

CELESTE: I don't like being sent for!

LE GENTIL: I know that, Celeste. That's precisely why I do it.

               She turns to him in surprise. He leans close.

LE GENTIL: I haven't slept a wink, have you?

CELESTE: No.

LE GENTIL: Why not?

CELESTE: Why not?

LE GENTIL: Is your bed not comfortable? Is the moon too bright?

CELESTE: I—

LE GENTIL: You have a guilty conscience, perhaps.

CELESTE: I was thinking about you!

LE GENTIL: Good. That's good, Celeste. But what were you thinking? Tell me, I want to know exactly.

CELESTE: Exactly?

LE GENTIL: Exactly. *(He watches her closely, laughs.)* Never mind, I have my answer. *(He moves away.)* You blush so prettily.

                She stands abruptly.

                There's no need to be embarrassed. At your age, if you didn't blush I'd be alarmed.

CELESTE: If you want to know what I was thinking, tonight, in my room, I was thinking how angry you make me, how careless you are towards me, how you never tell me things! Today, for instance—

LE GENTIL: Come, Celeste, be honest. You were going to be upset, no matter what I did, simply because I'm going away.

CELESTE: That's not true.

LE GENTIL: If I had come to you first thing, you would still have spent the day in tears.

CELESTE: I haven't been in tears.

LE GENTIL: Your eyes are red as rhubarb.

CELESTE: Maybe I was reading.

LE GENTIL: Were you?

CELESTE: Yes! Why not? Sometimes I do.

LE GENTIL: What about?

CELESTE: What about?

LE GENTIL: What were you reading about?

CELESTE: Astronomy! You don't believe me. You don't think I have the mind for it.

LE GENTIL: I've never said that.

CELESTE: Well, you don't talk to me about it, ever. You've never explained why it is you have to go, or where. Venus, India. India, Venus. What does that mean to me? I don't understand it and I don't see how it matters, next to me!

LE GENTIL: Then I'll explain it. Shall I do that now?

CELESTE: *(Hesitating.)* How long will it take?

              He laughs, then moves to the globe.

LE GENTIL: Come. We'll start on earth and work our way up. What's the matter? I'm only going to show you where I'm bound for.

              She moves marginally closer to the globe. He spins it with a practiced hand.

              This is France, you see? This little brown dot right here is Paris, which places us about here. You can move closer if you can't see.

CELESTE: *(Although she can't.)* I can see.

LE GENTIL: We sail from Brest. That's here. *(He traces the route with a finger.)* In three months, possibly four, we'll have rounded the Cape of Storms—here, at the southern tip of Africa—and put in at Île de France. We lay over there, then sail northeast to India, to one of our colonies, a little place called Pondichéry. That's here, below Madras. You're sure you can see?

CELESTE: Yes!

LE GENTIL: At Pondichéry I'll establish my observatory. *(He studies the globe.)* Tell me, Celeste, do you like the names?

CELESTE: Names?

LE GENTIL: All the names of places I've never seen, I like the
              sound of them. I imagine them like jewels, shining on
              the sea. I imagine I'll pluck them from the sea and
              wear them strung around my neck. That sounds
              foolish to you, I'm sure. The truth is, I've hungered all
              my life for travel, and I've hardly set foot outside of
              France. *(With his eyes on the globe.)* Your eyes are
              remarkable.

CELESTE: They are?

LE GENTIL: Oh yes. To see such detail from such a distance… is
              quite remarkable. *(He spins the globe, faces her, and
              grins.)* You're shivering. Come and sit down. I'll tuck
              my robe around you.

CELESTE: I'm all right.

LE GENTIL: You're shaking like a leaf. *(He moves to a chair.)* Sit.

              She obeys. He drapes his robe across her lap.

CELESTE: You'll be cold yourself.

LE GENTIL: I'm never cold.

              *He kneels to tuck the robe around her legs. She reaches
              out to touch his hair, but he catches her hand, kisses it
              lightly, and moves away.*

              Now, what else do you want to know? Next year on
              the sixth of June, for the first time in more than a
              century, Venus will pass across the face of the sun.
              I'm going to chart that passage. And my
              measurements—

CELESTE: It doesn't have to be you.

LE GENTIL: I beg your pardon?

CELESTE: Anyone can take those measurements. It doesn't have
              to be you.

LE GENTIL: Who told you that?

CELESTE: It's the truth, isn't it? You're not going because you have to go, you're going because you want to go!

LE GENTIL: It's a matter of timing, if you want to know. Timing, resources. Willingness.

CELESTE: Selfishness!

He studies her briefly, then moves a footstool close to her and sits.

LE GENTIL: I'm going to tell you something, Celeste—something that may surprise you. When I was eighteen, and my father was dying, he made me swear a solemn promise. He made me promise to become a priest. Me, Le Gentil, a priest! It was a source of some amusement to my friends, I can tell you. But I fully intended to keep that promise, I even began to study for the priesthood. And then one evening, quite by chance, I happened to hear a lecture by the great Delisle. He had just returned from Russia, from the court of Catherine the Great, where he had trained an entire generation of astronomers. I happened to hear him speak and as he spoke, something in the room… caught hold of me. Something caught hold of me, and in that moment my life was changed. The next morning, in spite of my promise to my father, I gave up the Church. I began to study astronomy. I knew, you see I was absolutely certain—I had found another, better way to devote myself to God.

CELESTE: I don't see what it has to do with God.

LE GENTIL: Then you don't see what I see when you look up at the sky.

CELESTE: And what is that?

LE GENTIL: A thousand mysteries, each more intricate than the last. Created by God for a purpose: to remind us of our mortality, to challenge and diminish us, to keep us hopeful, to keep us humble. No one, not the brightest savant nor the sauciest wisp of a girl, can possibly look at the sky and not be moved to wonder.

What a creation, Celeste. What a Creator! What a privilege to be one of a handful of men able to probe those mysteries, and by probing them, help to justify the ways of God to man. *(He stands.)* Now truthfully, Celeste. *(He moves in behind her.)* Do you imagine I would allow myself to be distracted from such magnificent endeavours by anything or any one? Least of all a little convent girl too stubborn to send me off to India with a smile. Come, I'm only teasing. If you did send me off with a smile, I'd probably wonder who you'd found to replace me.

CELESTE: I could never replace you!

LE GENTIL: That's right, you couldn't. Don't even consider it.

CELESTE: But you could replace me quite easily, I think.

LE GENTIL: Probably. If I chose to.

CELESTE: You really mean that, don't you?

               He laughs and takes her face in his hands.

LE GENTIL: Were you actually reading astronomy? The truth, now.

CELESTE: No.

LE GENTIL: *(Dropping his hands.)* I didn't think so.

CELESTE: I was reading about something much more interesting.

LE GENTIL: Oh? What's that?

CELESTE: Love.

LE GENTIL: Ah.

               He moves away.

CELESTE: You don't agree. You don't find love interesting. You find the sky interesting. Why? Because it's mysterious. Well, love is mysterious. You can't see it, even through a telescope. What could be more mysterious than that? What's the matter?

LE GENTIL: I'm listening. Go on. Explain it.

CELESTE: I just did!

LE GENTIL: *(Laughs.)* And so concisely.

CELESTE: *(Turning away.)* I can't explain it very well. It's too complicated.

LE GENTIL: What a shame. And I was just beginning to grow interested.

CELESTE: Besides, I'm not sure what to believe. There's romantic love, and that's one thing. And then there's what they call platonic love. I don't believe in that at all, do you?

LE GENTIL: I'm not sure.

CELESTE: You know what it is.

LE GENTIL: I know what it is.

CELESTE: You've heard of it, but never practiced it.

LE GENTIL: I've tried.

CELESTE: You've tried! What a mistake. This fellow I'm reading, in this book I found, he has it all figured out. He's even written a little poem. I'll recite it for you, if you like.
                (Reciting.) "Platonic love: a pretty name.
                But oh, it something odd is
                That lovers should each other view
                As if they had no bodies."

                She stares at him defiantly, and waits.

LE GENTIL: Well. That's coming to the point, red cheeks and all. *(He moves to her.)* All right, come on, let's go.

                He takes her hand and begins to lead her off.

CELESTE: What are you doing?

LE GENTIL: We can't do it here; I wouldn't recommend it. We'll have to find a bed.

CELESTE: I don't mean that, I don't mean—

LE GENTIL: Now?

CELESTE: Like this!

LE GENTIL: What's wrong with this?

CELESTE: Just—suddenly, because I ask you?

LE GENTIL: How do you want me to do it?

CELESTE: I want—*(She pulls away.)* Oh God, I can't stand it. I can't stand the way you always twist me around!

LE GENTIL: *(Laying a hand on her arm.)* Celeste—

CELESTE: *(Throwing off his hand.)* You pretend you don't understand, but you do. You understand perfectly!

LE GENTIL: Yes, all right, I understand. You want me to make love to you.

                Silence, which means yes.

                I don't think it's poetry you've been reading, I think it's novels. Don't you know what they say? No chaste girl has ever read novels. It's Monsieur Rousseau who says that, I believe. And he should know, since he's the one who writes them.

CELESTE: I've never read a novel in my life.

LE GENTIL: Good. Keep it that way. *(Beat.)* I can't do it, Celeste.

CELESTE: Once. just once, before you go.

LE GENTIL: No.

CELESTE: Why not?

LE GENTIL: You know why not.

CELESTE: Then marry me.

LE GENTIL: I will marry you, with great pleasure. When I return.

CELESTE: Now.

LE GENTIL: There isn't time.

CELESTE: Delay your departure.

LE GENTIL: I can't.

CELESTE: You have an answer for everything, don't you?!

                He moves abruptly away. Her manner changes.

                Don't you ever think about it?

LE GENTIL: I think about it all the time.

CELESTE: Then how do you stand it? *(She turns away.)* Don't
                look at me like that. I'm fine, I assure you. It's not for
                me that I suggest it.

LE GENTIL: You were thinking of me.

CELESTE: I was thinking—*(She breaks off.)*

LE GENTIL: Yes?

CELESTE: I was thinking you might like to have a baby.

LE GENTIL: I would, someday.

CELESTE: I meant a baby to come back to.

LE GENTIL: What kind of talk is this?

CELESTE: Would you like one?

LE GENTIL: No.

CELESTE: So definite! And what about me? What if I want one?

LE GENTIL: You're hardly more than a baby yourself.

CELESTE: What if I want one?

LE GENTIL: But you don't. Come, Celeste, you're only saying this
                because you're afraid.

CELESTE: Of what?

LE GENTIL: Of losing me.

CELESTE: How do you know that? *(She turns away.)* Oh, I wish I were more complicated!

LE GENTIL: You're complicated enough as you are.

CELESTE: No. *(Moving away.)* No, that's not true. What I need, what I really need to have is a mystery buried deep inside, a puzzle or conundrum that must be solved...and can't be solved too easily; that's important. But there's nothing like that, is there? There's nothing in me that understanding it would add in any way to any kind of knowledge. No reputations to be made or lost, no seas to sail to find it. So what hope do I have? What hope did I ever have? *(Beat.)* You're staring at me.

LE GENTIL: Am I?.

CELESTE: Like a cow at a new barn door.

LE GENTIL: Do you mind?

CELESTE: Yes!

LE GENTIL: That's unfortunate; I reserve the right to stare at you. How else am I going to decide?

CELESTE: Decide what?

LE GENTIL: Whether or not you're beautiful.

CELESTE: I can give you the answer to that. I'm not.

LE GENTIL: I think perhaps you are.

CELESTE: Oh no, I'm not...you do?

LE GENTIL moves abruptly to the telescope.

LE GENTIL: Come here, Celeste, I want to show you something.

He puts his eye to the telescope, adjusts it, pulls away.

CELESTE: I don't want to look at any of your cold stars!

LE GENTIL: Please.

She moves reluctantly to the telescope.

Look through that lens, and tell me what you see.

She obeys, but immediately pulls back.

Yes, I know, it's astonishing. Enough to stop the heart. Try again. What do you see?

CELESTE: A lot of stars.

LE GENTIL: And?

CELESTE: A great white ball.

LE GENTIL: Venus. Brightest object in the night sky, brighter even than the Moon. First star of the evening, last star of the morning—though not, in fact, a star at all but a planet. A milky-white luminous disk of a planet that gleams in the night sky like a star. No wonder men look at her and think of love. *(He is looking at CELESTE.)* No wonder men love.

     CELESTE pulls back from the telescope and turns to face him.

For the Babylonians, it was a luminous lion that roamed the night sky from east to west. But the great god El was jealous of its brightness, so every day at dawn he had it put to death. And every day at dusk the lion rose from the dead, to roam the skies again. For the Mesopotamians, it was the goddess Ishtar, queen of the heavens, daughter of the moon. She was a lot like you, this Ishtar. She was young, beautiful— or not beautiful, if you insist. She was impulsive, and quite contradictory. In fact, she was the goddess of contradictory forces: fire and fire-quenching, fair play and enmity, rejoicing and tears. She was often seen in the company of a lion, and when the lion roared—well, that was thunder. For certain cultures in Africa, she was both the evening and the morning star, the wives of the moon, sometimes the sister of the sun. For the Greeks, she was Aphrodite, goddess of love; for the Romans, Venus. And for me—

Guillaume Joseph Hyacinthe Jean Baptiste Le Gentil de la Galasière—*(Executing a mock bow.)*—she is destiny. What's the matter?

CELESTE: The way you talk…

LE GENTIL: Do you like it? *(He moves very close.)* If you like it, I'll fill your days with it, and your nights as well. I'll tell you all about the stars and the moon and the planets, and you'll tell me about love. And when we've exhausted those subjects, if we ever do, we can argue about how beautiful you are. But not yet, Celeste. First I go after Venus. Then I come back to you.

They stare at one another; no one moves.

Will you wait for me? Can you trust me, and do it? You can, I know you can, I can read it in your eyes. My God, Celeste, isn't it incredible? With all the things there are to look at in the world, that my eye should fall on you!

In the distance, church bells are heard.

CELESTE: I'm so afraid!

LE GENTIL: Hush! Listen to the bells.

CELESTE: Promise me you won't forget the little face of Celeste.

LE GENTIL: How could I?

He touches her face.

CELESTE: Promise me you'll come back.

LE GENTIL: Oh, I'll come back. God willing.

CELESTE: Don't say that! Don't ever say that.

LE GENTIL: *(Laughs.)* Why not, you silly girl?

CELESTE: I don't think it's absolutely certain God approves of us.

LE GENTIL: What kind of talk is that? Wasn't it God who brought us together in the first place?

CELESTE: I don't know.

LE GENTIL: Of course it was.

CELESTE: Why?

LE GENTIL: Why did He bring us together? Maybe He couldn't resist it.

                He smiles; she doesn't.

                Go back to your bed, Celeste. Sleep, and dream of me. Can you do that? Can you dream about me while I'm gone?

CELESTE: Yes.

LE GENTIL: Then I'll be with you every night. What more can we ask, than that?

                She stares at him, then turns and runs off.

                End of Act One.

Act Two

Scene One

The sitting room. 9:00 p.m. The windows are open. There are flowers everywhere. Near a chair by a window stands an ornate wooden chest. MME SYLVIE, dressed in her best but with a cane at her side, is asleep in a chair. Somewhere in the house, a clock strikes. MARGOT enters, in a simple dress. She is quite agitated but collects herself and moves to MME SYLVIE.

MARGOT: *(Softly.)* Madame?

Seeing that MME SYLVIE is asleep, MARGOT gently adjusts her shawl. She moves to a table, adjusts something there. She picks up her sewing, weighs it, throws it down. She moves to the windows and peers out. She sighs, turns back into the room. Her eyes fall on the chest. She glances at MME SYLVIE, then sits in front of the chest and, with a gentleness verging on reverence, lifts the lid. She takes out a sheet of paper and begins to read.

Camisoles, three dozen. Petticoats, two dozen. Underpetticoats, two dozen. Chemises, three dozen. Night shifts, eleven. Night caps, four. Negligées, seven. Dressing gowns, three.

Meanwhile, MME SYLVIE has awakened; she's been watching MARGOT in silence. Now she notices a fly on the arm of her chair. She coaxes it into the air and, as MARGOT resumes reading, picks up a wooden fly swatter in the shape of a book and begins to track the fly.

Stockings, twelve dozen. Summer gowns, fourteen. Winter gowns, eleven. Bonnets, eight. Shawls, seven. Lace, nine yards. Ribbon, eleven yards. Handkerchiefs—

> *MME SYLVIE claps the book to. The sound is like a crack of thunder in the room.*

Merciful heavens!

MME SYLVIE: Sorry. I couldn't resist a try.

MARGOT: And?

MME SYLVIE: *(Opening the fly-swatter.)* Missed him!

MARGOT: Again.

> *MARGOT closes the chest and stands.*

MME SYLVIE: There must be a trick to this.

MARGOT: Personally, Madame, if I had to choose between a houseful of flies and that thing clapping-to all day, I would choose the flies.

MME SYLVIE: Celeste seems to manage it well enough. I'll have to get her to teach me. *(She sets the fly swatter aside.)* Was I dreaming, or did I hear a clock?

MARGOT: It's just gone nine.

MME SYLVIE: Nine! Surely not.

MARGOT: You've been dead to the world, Madame. How you can sleep at a time like this—

MME SYLVIE: Will he get here any sooner if I stay awake? *(She puts on her spectacles.)* You were going to check on Demarais.

MARGOT: I did.

MME SYLVIE: And?

> *MME SYLVIE takes up her sewing.*

MARGOT: He's up and about.

MME SYLVIE: Well! He's feeling better, then.

                No response. MME SYLVIE looks up.

                Margot?

MARGOT: Can I fetch you something to eat, Madame? A little
                soup, perhaps? Some figs?

MME SYLVIE: Figs. Honestly, Margot—

MARGOT: It's only a suggestion.

MME SYLVIE: If I feel like something to eat, I promise you I'll have
                the temerity to ask for it.

                *MME SYLVIE resumes her work. MARGOT turns
                away but continues to hover.*

                I wish you'd tell me what's bothering you.

MARGOT: It's all this waiting, Madame. Every hour seems
                longer than the last.

MME SYLVIE: I'm sure we'll find there's a very good explanation.

MARGOT: That's what you said at five o'clock. And at seven. We
                won't keep her in that dress forever, you know. If he
                doesn't get here soon—

MME SYLVIE: He'll get here soon. Any minute now he'll come
                striding through the door, just as though he'd never
                been away!

MARGOT: You never doubt him, do you?

MME SYLVIE: Why should I?

MARGOT: Why indeed.

                *MARGOT moves to the window. MME SYLVIE lets
                her work fall.*

MME SYLVIE: I did sometimes wonder…

MARGOT: Madame?

MME SYLVIE: If I would ever get him back. I wondered if God
                 would grant me that, and what the price would be.
                 (Resuming her work.) He is an old gypsy, you know—
                 that God of yours. He seems to feel compelled to
                 always take with one hand while giving with the
                 other. You've noticed that, I'm sure.

MARGOT: Oh, Madame.

MME SYLVIE: No, you won't admit it, but it's true. He'll give me
                 back my son, perhaps, and take away my mind. My
                 poor embattled mind! Or give me a grandchild—how
                 I'd love a grandchild!—and find something equally
                 precious to deprive me of. He will; you watch. I've
                 been sparring with Him long enough to know this.
                 Well? Nothing to say?

MARGOT: *(Moving downstage.)* I know you like to pretend that
                 you're a cynic—

MME SYLVIE: Pretend?

MARGOT: And I know you like to bait me. What more is there to
                 say?

MME SYLVIE: *(Sighs.)* You were much more entertaining, Margot,
                 when you knew me less. I can see I'll have to look
                 elsewhere now for entertainment. Where's Celeste?

MARGOT: In the garden.

MME SYLVIE: Lord help us. More flowers!

MARGOT: Yes. It breaks my heart the way she counts on him.

MME SYLVIE: Well, of course she counts on him. What's got into
                 you? just because the man's a few hours late.

MARGOT: A few hours, a few years, it's all the same to him. He
                 does exactly as he likes; he always has. He never stops
                 to think—

                 MME SYLVIE stiffens.

MME SYLVIE: You know very well why he's been away so long.

MARGOT: Yes.

MME SYLVIE: And you know why he's late today. It's those scientists at the Academy. They've held him up, poring over all his studies—

MARGOT: Forgive me, Madame. I shouldn't have said that.

MME SYLVIE: I have to say I'm disappointed. I used to sense it in you often, this festering distrust of him. I thought you'd laid all that to rest.

MARGOT: I have, Madame—through the grace of God.

MME SYLVIE: You *had*, you mean…until that boy returned.

               MARGOT turns away.

               He's said something, hasn't he?

MARGOT: No, Madame.

MME SYLVIE: If he's said something that concerns my son, I have a right to know. Margot?

MARGOT: It's not so much what he's said as what he won't say. He won't speak for Le Gentil, not on any issue.

MME SYLVIE: Well, of course he won't. He shouldn't.

MARGOT: But he's so evasive! He won't supply a simple "yes" or "no" to anything I ask. He seems reluctant to look me in the eye, and when he does—(*She breaks off.*) He makes me fearful. I can't help it, he makes me fearful for Celeste.

MME SYLVIE: And what else? Come, I know there's more.

MARGOT: You're mistaken, Madame.

MME SYLVIE: Do me a favour, Margot, would you? Don't tell me lies, not even little white ones. The last thing I want to have to think of when I go to bed at night is you on your knees to the Lord, begging forgiveness for some silly little fib!

MARGOT sits.

MARGOT: He said your son is bound to disappoint.

MME SYLVIE: He said what?

MARGOT: I asked Demarais if there was any danger that your son would disappoint Celeste, and he said he is bound to.

MME SYLVIE: Bound to?

MARGOT: That's what he said, Madame. That was the most he'd say, and that was all of it.

MME SYLVIE is visibly shaken.

MME SYLVIE: What a world we live in! Who can explain it? We rise up from the banquet table, and drop dead of hunger.

MARGOT: Now I've upset you.

MME SYLVIE: Life upsets me. There's nothing new in that. Bound to, you say?

MARGOT: I didn't want to worry you, Madame—

MME SYLVIE: What does that mean, anyway—bound to? That's a cryptic phrase, if ever I heard one.

MARGOT: As I say, he's quite evasive.

MME SYLVIE: It means nothing, that phrase. I'd dismiss it out of hand, if I were you. As a matter of fact, I'm surprised you haven't. *(A definite dig.)* You need to have a little faith, Margot.

MARGOT: Perhaps. I may not be a skeptic when it comes to God, but when it comes to man…

MME SYLVIE: *(Pause.)* If he disappoints Celeste, Margot, he disappoints us all.

MARGOT: I know.

MME SYLVIE: He won't do it. I don't believe it for a minute. He may not be perfect, my son, but he is steadfast; that much I know. He's written to her faithfully, all this time—

MARGOT: That's true.

MME SYLVIE: Which is more than we can say for Celeste.

MARGOT: That's true, as well.

MME SYLVIE: A man who persists in writing to a girl too proud to reply is not the kind of man who disappoints. Especially...especially when he's so proud himself. Oh God, Margot. She may have lost him, doing that. I said it! I said it all along.

MARGOT: I beg your pardon?

MME SYLVIE: I warned her.

MARGOT: On the contrary, Madame. You encouraged her.

MME SYLVIE: I did nothing of the kind!

MARGOT: You did, you know. She asked how you would feel if she were to stop writing to him, and you said that while you couldn't condone it as a mother, as a *woman*—

MME SYLVIE: *(Hastily.)* If I said that, I don't remember. You know very well, my memory—

MARGOT: Your memory is remarkable, Madame... when it needs to be.

MME SYLVIE: *(Looking at MARGOT in surprise.)* Well, well, well! She retaliates. That's a change of pace.

> CELESTE *enters, carrying flowers. Her dress is exquisite. MARGOT and MME SYLVIE quickly take up their work. CELESTE moves to a table, sets the flowers in a vase, and begins to arrange them.*

CELESTE: You're very quiet, the two of you. Have you been talking about me?

MME SYLVIE: Heavens! Such conceit.

MARGOT: More flowers, Celeste? The room is like a garden.

CELESTE: I know; I like it. It looks *gemutlich*, as the Germans say.

MME SYLVIE: It may look *gemutlich*, but it smells like a perfumery. And what's more this fly-thing of yours doesn't work.

MARGOT: It works well enough, I think, when the worker is a little slyer than the fly.

MME SYLVIE: Oh, is that what's required. *(To CELESTE.)* I take it there's no sign of him.

CELESTE: None.

MME SYLVIE: *(Reaching for her cane.)* Well, I don't know why I should be so impatient. At least we know that he's in France. That's a consolation, isn't it. *(She stands with some difficulty.)* He's not off on some desolate island—

MARGOT: Or bobbing like a cork in the middle of the sea.

CELESTE: They're not desolate, those islands. They're lush and verdant. They smell of jasmine, and frangipane. I wish I knew what that was like! And at night, the sky drops down around them like a great bejeweled bowl.

MME SYLVIE: *(Sighs.)* He does write a lovely letter.

                MME SYLVIE moves slowly towards the windows.

CELESTE: He does.

                She carries the vase to another table, sets it down.

                I didn't get that from a letter, though. I got it from a book.

MARGOT: You and your books. If you'd spent half the time on housework that you've spent on books—

MME SYLVIE: Oh, she can always learn housework.

MARGOT: And needlework, too, I suppose?

MME SYLVIE: If she's going to wear her eyes out, let her do it on words.

MARGOT: I know you feel that way, Madame. You've often said it. When, in fact, if you'd supported me in this—

MME SYLVIE: *(Sharply.)* If I'd supported you, what would we have? Two excellent seamstresses, when clearly all we need is one!

> *MME SYLVIE turns away. MARGOT picks up her work and makes a show of doing it.*

CELESTE: This is because of him, isn't it? Because he's late. *(To MARGOT.)* All your preparations—

MARGOT: There's nothing that won't keep.

CELESTE: The food—

MARGOT: The food will taste just as good tomorrow as it did today.

CELESTE: You've worn yourself out, looking after Demarais. *(She turns to MME SYLVIE.)* And you've hardly slept at all.

MME SYLVIE: Since when?

CELESTE: Since we got word that they'd reached France.

MME SYLVIE: Nonsense.

CELESTE: I know you, Madame.

MME SYLVIE: I have slept like a newborn babe!

CELESTE: Well! Everything's fine, then. What a relief.

> *CELESTE turns to leave.*

MME SYLVIE: Where are you going?

CELESTE: For a walk.

MARGOT: You're not!

MME SYLVIE:　Always running out on us!

CELESTE:　　I can't sit here, twiddling my thumbs. You know that.

MARGOT:　　That's no reason to go wandering through the fields in that dress—

MME SYLVIE:　At this hour.

CELESTE:　　All right, I'll change.

She starts off again.

MARGOT:　　Oh no! He could arrive at any moment, Celeste.

CELESTE:　　Well, if he does, I'd just as soon he didn't know that I've spent the entire day looking like this.

MME SYLVIE:　Celeste! Your mother went to so much trouble.

MARGOT:　　Never mind, Madame. She's been waiting all along for an excuse to do this.

CELESTE:　　That's not true.

MARGOT:　　She didn't want to wear it in the first place. She finds it overdone, you see.

CELESTE:　　That's not what I said.

MARGOT:　　No, you said—

CELESTE:　　I didn't want to look as though I was trying to impress him. That's all I meant.

MME SYLVIE:　That's a very strange attitude.

CELESTE:　　Is it?

MME SYLVIE:　Towards the man you're going to marry? I should say so.

CELESTE:　　Well, this is an improvement. Now you're picking on me instead of one another!

Silence.

MME SYLVIE: You're quite right, Celeste. We are behaving badly.

CELESTE: Why, Madame?

MME SYLVIE: Why? Well—

MARGOT: It's my fault, Celeste. I take the blame entirely. And if you want to change, by all means go and do it. It's silly to be quarrelling about a dress.

CELESTE moves to MARGOT.

CELESTE: Please understand. It's not that I dislike it; how could I? It's exquisite.

MARGOT: *(Touching her face.)* I just want you to look beautiful! Is that so strange?

CELESTE: But that's the point. He's seen so much beauty in the world. I don't want to took as though I'm trying to compete.

MARGOT: Compete? *(To MME SYLVIE.)* Listen to her.

CELESTE: I'd feel more comfortable, I think, in something a little simpler. Something more like yours.

MARGOT: For his coming-home?

CELESTE: To me this seems almost like a wedding gown.

MARGOT: It's not at all like a wedding gown. Is it, Madame. Tell her. She'll listen to you.

MME SYLVIE doesn't reply. She is staring out the window. The sky is ablaze with colour.

Madame?

MME SYLVIE: Look at it, would you? Did you ever in your life see a day so…

CELESTE: Lovely!

MME SYLVIE: I was going to say, so French. *(She faces MARGOT.)* She has to know, Margot.

MARGOT: Madame—

MME SYLVIE: How can we send her into battle utterly unarmed?

CELESTE: What are you talking about? Madame?

MME SYLVIE: *(Moving downstage.)* I'm talking about Demarais.

CELESTE: What about him?

MARGOT: Oh, Madame.

MME SYLVIE: Your mother, you see. Just before you came in, your mother was as cranky as a wall bug. So in the end we had a quarrel—over something that he said.

CELESTE: Demarais? *(To MARGOT.)* I thought he wasn't well enough to talk.

MARGOT: He's not. That is, he wasn't, but—

CELESTE: You said he was delirious.

MARGOT: He was, Celeste, at first. And then, for a few days, he refused to talk at all.

CELESTE: But now he's talking. What does he say? It's about Le Gentil, isn't it? What is it? Is something wrong?

MARGOT: Now listen, Celeste. We mustn't jump to conclusions.

CELESTE: *(To MME SYLVIE.)* Madame?

MME SYLVIE: Ask him yourself. He's up and about, apparently.

> *CELESTE starts off. MARGOT stands.*

MARGOT: Celeste! Don't upset him. He's not as well as he pretends to be. Celeste?

> *CELESTE exits. MARGOT sinks back into her chair.*
> *MME SYLVIE moves next to her.*

MME SYLVIE: You probably think I shouldn't have done that. Where the devil cannot go, he sends an old woman. That's what you're thinking.

MARGOT: *(With difficulty.)* I pray every night, Madame, for the
              courage to let her go. Simply...to let her go. Why
              should that be so difficult? It sounds so easy. *(She
              turns away.)* I envy you your strength, Madame.

MME SYLVIE: I envy you your faith.

MARGOT: *(Looking up in surprise.)* You've never said that before.

MME SYLVIE: And I never shall again. Come, give me your hand. I
              feel the need of it.

              MARGOT obeys.

              We're condemned to rely on them, aren't we, you and
              I? We were condemned to it the day that they were
              born. I have to say I find that onerous, at times. I'd
              prefer to be independent.

              *MME SYLVIE grips MARGOT's hand more tightly
              and turns toward the window.*

              She has a way of taking the sun with her, have you
              noticed that? When she leaves a room?

Scene Two

              *The study; immediately following. DEMARAIS leans
              over a table, studying a map which is criss-crossed
              with ribbons and dotted with flags. CELESTE runs
              on, but stops when she sees him. There's an instant of
              confusion, then recognition.*

DEMARAIS: Celeste! I wouldn't have known you.

CELESTE: I wouldn't have known you. You didn't use to be so—
              tall.

DEMARAIS: So thin, you mean. Well, I'm not as thin as I was a few
              days ago; your mother has seen to that. Where are
              you off to?

CELESTE: Oh, I—came to see you.

DEMARAIS: *(On his guard.)* Oh?

CELESTE: Yes, they—told me you were out of bed.

DEMARAIS: Did they? They were right.

CELESTE: I would have been to see you sooner, but I was told that you weren't well enough to talk. Are you well enough?

DEMARAIS: I think so.

CELESTE: Good. I'm glad to hear it, Demarais. We've been worried about you. My mother—(*She breaks off.*) My mother in particular has been worried.

DEMARAIS: She certainly has.

                An awkward pause.

CELESTE: I see you've been studying my map.

DEMARAIS: You made this? When?

CELESTE: As the letters arrived.

DEMARAIS: Explain it to me.

CELESTE: It's as simple as it looks. (*She moves closer.*) The ribbons are the voyages, the flags the ports of call. Each colour represents a different year.

DEMARAIS: Red is the first year; that's obvious. And green must be the second—

CELESTE: The year he missed the transit. You'll notice there's not a single flag on India! Then white and blue: dozens of ribbons and as many flags—

DEMARAIS: All those wretched excursions.

CELESTE: (*Letting this pass.*) The fifth year is yellow and the sixth magenta. Magenta is the colour that brought him home! If I'd known that, I would have used it sooner. I'm sorry. I shouldn't talk as though you weren't there with him.

DEMARAIS: But I wasn't. I was on another journey altogether.

CELESTE: He said you hadn't taken all that well to the sea.

DEMARAIS: *(With a mirthless laugh.)* Yes. He would put it like that. *(He turns back to the map.)* Tell me something. Why did you do this?

CELESTE: It was a way of going with him. I feel as though I've followed him everywhere, like a shadow. I have other maps, where I've done latitudes and longitudes. Trade winds, navigational routes. Everything he studied and observed. Flora, fauna, soils. Winds and tides; monsoons.

DEMARAIS: *(Genuinely astounded.)* How did you learn all this?

CELESTE: From his letters. And from books. I've read every book in the house, I think, and any I could beg from the curé. History, geography, philosophy. Letters. Even a little astronomy. The more I learned, the more I found I had to learn, and the more mysterious the world became.

DEMARAIS: Does he know about this?

CELESTE: I wanted to surprise him.

DEMARAIS: He'll be surprised, all right. I'm surprised! I used to try and picture you, from time to time, while I was away—as I pictured many things in France. *(Indicating the map.)* But I never once pictured you doing this.

CELESTE: What was I doing?

DEMARAIS: I—oh, I don't know. Feminine things.

                She stiffens. He studies the map, unaware that he's offended her.

CELESTE: Do something for me, Demarais. Tell me about the sea.

DEMARAIS: The sea.

CELESTE: I like to try and picture it, in all its splendour.

DEMARAIS: In that case, I suggest you wait for Le Gentil. *(With an edge.)* He's much better than I am at splendour.

CELESTE: I would love to see the sea. I would love to sail it.

DEMARAIS: You would never survive.

CELESTE: I might surprise you, Demarais.

DEMARAIS: Believe me, you would not survive the sea. That takes a kind of madness.

CELESTE: You survived it.

DEMARAIS: I lived. That's a different thing.

CELESTE: What about the sailors?

DEMARAIS: Mad. All mad.

CELESTE: And Le Gentil?

DEMARAIS: He's the maddest of the lot.

              CELESTE laughs.

              You don't believe me?

CELESTE: Of course not.

DEMARAIS: You've been with him, have you? All this time?

CELESTE: I have his letters. He did write to me, you know. One hundred and sixty-two letters! Every one of them as rich as a tapestry.

DENLARAIS: Oh, well then. You have nothing to learn from me.

              DEMARAIS picks up a book and flips through it.

CELESTE: I wouldn't go that far, Demarais—

DEMARAIS: No.

CELESTE: But I know he isn't mad! Unless he's changed beyond all recognition. Has he changed?

DEMJUWS: We've all changed, haven't we?

CELESTE: For the better, I would hope.

DEMARAIS: Who can say?

                 DEMARAIS replaces the book and picks up another.

CELESTE: Is he—as handsome as he was?

DEMARAIS: I'm hardly an authority on that.

CELESTE: You could venture an opinion.

DEMARAIS: You could wait a while, and find out for yourself

                 He replaces the book, then moves to the window.

CELESTE: He hasn't been ill. Has he?

DEMARAIS: Why ask me? You're the one with all the letters. One
                 hundred and sixty-two!

CELESTE: He might have kept it from me, if he had been ill. So
                 that I wouldn't worry.

DEMARAIS: *(With an abrupt, violent gesture.)* Oh, for the love of
                 Christ! Say what you've come to say, would you?
                 Then leave me the hell alone. *(Turns on her.)* I know
                 why you're here. Do you want to know how I know?
                 Because you behave exactly like your mother.
                 Sniffing around me like a shark who's—*(He sways,
                 reaches for support.)*—scented—

CELESTE: *(Moving to him.)* Sit down.

DEMARAIS: Merciful Christ!

CELESTE: Sit down, until it passes.

                 *She helps him to a chair, pours a drink for him from a
                 carafe, and sits next to him.*

                 Put your head back. You'll feel better in a minute.

DEMARAIS: My God, you know, I'm—*(He breaks off.)*

CELESTE: What?

DEMARAIS: I'm terrified I'll never get over this!

CELESTE: *(Taking his hand.)* You'll get over it.

DEMARAIS: I wonder.

CELESTE: You will. Especially if you don't have to contend with me.

DEMARAIS: I should have stayed in bed.

CELESTE: Perhaps.

DEMARAIS: I was sick to death of my own thoughts! I haven't had a conversation since I got here. No one comes to see me. Not even you.

CELESTE: I was forbidden to.

DEMARAIS: You do as you're told now, do you?

CELESTE: Sometimes.

DEMARAIS: Sometimes?

CELESTE: When I must.

                She smiles.

DEMARAIS: That's better. I was beginning to think that frown had molded itself to your forehead. *(He studies her.)* He's going to be amazed, you know. There was hardly anything to you when we went away. Now you're quite, quite—grown.

CELESTE: Do you think he'll be pleased?

DEMARAIS: Oh, I—don't see why not.

CELESTE: You don't see why not. Try to restrain your enthusiasm, Demarais—

DEMARAIS: It's not my place to tell you that you're beautiful. *(He turns away.)* He's a lucky man.

CELESTE: Not so lucky perhaps. He missed the transit, didn't he?

DEMARAIS: That was my fault. Oh, I know he'd never say that,

but it's true. We couldn't get to Pondichéry; it was
under siege. But we might have sailed to Java. He
could have charted the transit there. But I was ill—I
was eternally ill—and he refused to leave me.

CELESTE: Oh, Demarais.

DEMARAIS: I was a weight around his neck from the moment we
left France. I was sick at sea, and sicker still on land. I
was homesick; I was lonely; I was scared to death. He
never said it, he never once reproached me or
complained. But I could feel his expectations for me
fading with each day. You're shocked, aren't you?

CELESTE: No.

DEMARAIS: You are. I can see it in your face.

CELESTE: I can't believe that none of it was any good. I can't
believe that! There must be something you enjoyed.
There must be one good memory.

DEMARAIS: *(After a moment.)* I do remember one afternoon. We
were somewhere off the coast of Africa. One of the
sailors fell head first from the crow's-nest into the sea.
I asked him what made him come down and he said,
"Common sense."

             He laughs, this time with genuine mirth.

I liked that. I like—little things. Le Gentil, you know,
he likes things vast. Me, I like them small. I like to be
able to reach a thing and hold it in my hand.

             He finds himself staring at her hand; he raises his eyes.

That's a remarkable dress you're wearing.

CELESTE: Is it.

DEMARAIS: A dress like that makes a man feel very welcome.

             She pulls her hand away, and stands.

What's the matter? What did I say?

CELESTE: Nothing.

              She moves to the window.

DEMARAIS: I wasn't referring to myself—

CELESTE: I know!

DEMARAIS: You have a great capacity for anger, haven't you? I don't think I'd want to be the one who usually inspires it.

CELESTE: I'm not angry with you, Demarais. I'm angry because I'm stuck here in this—fluffy, fluffy gown, waiting for a man who's always late. *(She opens the window.)* Look, it's almost dark out now. Will he arrive at all tonight? Or will I have to make do with another dream. Oh, Demarais. I can't begin to tell you how tired I am of dreams.

DEMARAIS: I understand that.

CELESTE: Do you? I wonder. I wonder what you'd say if I were to tell you that I've dreamed of him every night since he's been gone.

DEMARAIS: I'd say that's—quite a feat.

CELESTE: The curé doesn't approve. He thinks I should dream of salvation. I dream of Le Gentil. And in the morning, do you know what I do? I open the little chest where I keep his letters and read them all again. I've committed them to memory! But I read them anyway because I like to study the handwriting, to imagine him forming each letter. Everything he touches, everything his eye falls on is beautiful to me. Do you think that's wrong?

DEMARAIS: Not necessarily.

CELESTE: The curé does. The curé has for some time denied me the Holy Sacrament—because of Le Gentil.

DEMARAIS: Listen to me, Celeste. I know how you feel because there was a time when I felt much the same. I wanted to be like him in every way, to stride across the world with all that energy and optimism. To light a fire in everyone I met. But I've learned—I've learned that only God is perfect, and that it's wrong to look for God in Le Gentil. It's wrong, Celeste, and what's more it's not fair. To him, or to you.

CELESTE: What are you saying?

DEMARAIS: He's a man, like any other—

CELESTE: He's not like any other.

DEMARAIS: He's a man. Sometimes he'll exceed your expectations; sometimes he'll fall short. If you expect it to be otherwise—*(He breaks off.)* Don't expect it to be otherwise.

He pulls himself out of his chair.

CELESTE: Where are you going?

DEMARAIS: Back to bed.

CELESTE: Now? You say this, and then walk away.?

DEMARAIS: I can't say any more. There was a time I wouldn't have said this much. There was a time you couldn't have pried a word against him from my mouth. But I've come to see the world for what it is, and I know that sometimes—sometimes!—there's more beauty in a little act of kindness than in all the splendour of the universe.

DEMARAIS starts off.

CELESTE: You think you've done this out of kindness? You're fooling yourself It's not kindness, Demarais, it's jealousy. You're jealous of him, because you know in your heart that you're not like him at all!

He faces her.

DEMARAIS: That's right. That's absolutely right. I'm not like him, at all. At first, when I first understood that, I thought

I'd die of shame. Not anymore. Because I've decided that God planned for this. He knew all along there'd be little men, as well as great. He made room in His heart for both. After all, if He could imagine the universe, He could certainly imagine me!

DEMARAIS exits. CELESTE stares after him. Then she moves to the window and closes it. She moves to the map and covers it with a cloth. Finally she starts off, but as she nears the stairs leading to the observatory, she stops moving and turns towards them, as though drawn by an irresistible force.

Scene Three

The observatory and the stairs leading up to it. Immediately following. CELESTE climbs the stairs and enters the observatory. A window is open; the curtains billow into the room. She closes the window. LE GENTIL steps out of the shadows.

LE GENTIL: I thought you'd never come.

CELESTE: Le Gentil?

LE GENTIL: In the flesh.

He moves to the desk and lights a candle.

CELESTE: How long have you been here?

LE GENTIL: Hours.

CELESTE: Hours! But we've—

LE GENTIL: Come here by the light. I want to look at you.

CELESTE: We've been waiting for you!

LE GENTIL: Like vultures, I know. *(He lifts the candle.)* Come to the light, Celeste. You're not afraid, are you?

CELESTE: Of course not.

She steps into the light.

LE GENTIL: My God! Who would believe it? Right in the heart of France.

CELESTE: What do you mean? What do you mean by that? And why do you call us vultures?

LE GENTIL sets down the candle, and begins to move restlessly around the room.

LE GENTIL: This room! It's like a dream to me. And everything that happened here, a dream. We said goodbye here, didn't we? I seem to remember.

CELESTE: You seem to remember?

LE GENTIL: No, no, I remember. There was moonlight, wasn't there? It washed the room. You came to me half-dressed, and half-asleep. You begged me to seduce you.

CELESTE: Did I?

LE GENTIL: Oh yes, you came right out with it. I liked that. Damn near did it, too. You look confused. How could you forget these things? It's not so long ago.

CELESTE: Only six years!

LE GENTIL: Seems like yesterday to me. How is my mother?

CELESTE: Your—

LE GENTIL: Mother, yes.

CELESTE: She's waiting for you. She's waited patiently for hours. We expected you at four, you see. We had everything planned.

LE GENTIL: I'm sure you did. There's an odour of expectation in this place—not just in it, all around. I got wind of it as far away as Paris. Did you always stand like that?

CELESTE: Like what?

LE GENTIL: Never mind. Tell me about Demarais. Is he better?

CELESTE: He's—improving, I would say.

LE GENTIL: Good. Good for now, at least. He'll likely have a relapse, maybe several; that's the pattern. Your hair is different, isn't it? Darker. Or have you changed the style?

CELESTE: It's—

LE GENTIL: Darker, I would say. Sit down.

CELESTE: I beg your pardon?

LE GENTIL: I said sit down.

                He begins to remove his jacket.

CELESTE: I don't want to sit down.

LE GENTIL: Do it anyway.

CELESTE: Why should I?

LE GENTIL: Because I want you to. There's something about your attitude, the way you stand, the way you hold your arms. I don't care for it.

CELESTE: You don't—

LE GENTIL: Care for it.

                He tosses his jacket across a chair.

CELESTE: I don't give a damn if you care for it or not!

                He turns back to her.

                I don't know who you think you are, I don't know what you think you're doing. But if you expect me to stand here and put up with this—

LE GENTIL: Not at all. I expect you to sit here and put up with it.

                She turns to leave.

                Celeste!

                He moves so that he can see her face.

                I had to do something, you looked so serious, as

though the end of the world were at hand. It's not the end of the world for you, is it—my coming home?

CELESTE: Of course not.

LE GENTIL: Then why do you look as though it is?

CELESTE: You seem so different—

LE GENTIL: In what way?

CELESTE: In every way! Your looks, your manner. I wasn't expecting you to—

LE GENTIL: What?

CELESTE: Behave like this!

LE GENTIL: And how do I behave?

CELESTE: Oh! You're not going to pretend that you don't know.

LE GENTIL: I don't.

CELESTE: You're constantly interrupting me. I've hardly been able to finish a single sentence! You leap from one subject to another—(She breaks off.) What are you grinning about?

LE GENTIL: Nothing.

CELESTE: I don't find any of this amusing.

LE GENTIL: I know. Go on, Celeste. I'm listening.

CELESTE: I can't remember a time in this house when we've been able to have a conversation that didn't eventually, no matter what it was, come back to you. I can't remember an hour when your name wasn't mentioned. In six solid years, not one of us has gone to sleep at night without praying for your safety. And you come home, come sneaking home like a thief in the night, and call us vultures?

LE GENTIL: That was unfair.

CELESTE: It was more than unfair; it was cruel. We don't deserve that, any of us. And we don't deserve to have our plans thrown in our faces. Imagine hiding up here, all this time. Hours, you say! While we've—

LE GENTIL: It wasn't hours. I don't know how long it's been; not hours. I wanted to see you alone, Celeste. Is that so hard to understand? My God, I've dreamt this night with you a thousand times. Why would I want to share it?

CELESTE: That still doesn't explain why you'd call us vultures.

LE GENTIL: You mustn't take offence at that. It has nothing to do with you, it comes of feeling suddenly—caged. You have to try to think of what I'm used to, what I've had the blessed fortune to grow used to.

CELESTE: And what's that?

LE GENTIL: Infinity! Infinity, Celeste. No end to anything, in any direction—east, south, north, west, up, down, anywhere! Can you imagine it? Can you imagine what it does to a man's soul? When I left here, I thought I had some measure of the mind of God, I thought I knew what vastness was, and distance, density—all those things. I was naïve. Every day I was away I learned anew, and with a kind of fresh surprise, how infinite is the mind of God, how intricate and how varied. And now I'm back, and everywhere I look I'm seeing walls and roofs and— limits. Even the land has a way of closing in on me. You can understand that, can't you?

CELESTE: I think so.

LE GENTIL: Good. I was hoping that you could. Come here. Come here, Celeste. *(He laughs.)* You're not going to do it, are you?

CELESTE: No.

LE GENTIL: You won't sit down when you're told to, you won't come to me when you're called. What am I to understand from this?

CELESTE: I'm not a little girl anymore.

LE GENTIL: I can see that.

CELESTE: I won't be led around by the nose.

LE GENTIL: Is that how you remember it?

CELESTE: Precisely.

LE GENTIL: And I remember it the other way around. I remember being led by the nose. What do you make of that? One of us has to be wrong. *(He moves to her and takes her hand.)* Have a little pity on me, Celeste. No matter how we began, it wouldn't be as you'd imagined. I was bound to disappoint you. Wasn't I?

CELESTE: Not necessarily.

LE GENTIL: Yes, I was, and I'll tell you why. You were expecting someone else. Someone pale and sappy and sentimental. Why deny it? It's what comes of reading all those novels.

CELESTE: I don't read novels

LE GENTIL: Don't look for a story-book suitor. You won't find him in me.

CELESTE: The last thing on this earth I want—believe me!—is a story-book suitor.

LE GENTIL: Good! I'm glad to hear it. What do you want?

CELESTE: *(Fervently.)* A real one.

LE GENTIL: In that case, you must expect some imperfections. Am I right?

CELESTE: Of course.

LE GENTIL: *(Beat.)* Your hair *is* darker, I'm convinced of it. It looks as rich as sable. *(He touches her hair.)* What are you thinking? Tell me.

CELESTE: You don't look at all like I remember.

LE GENTIL: Are you afraid of me?

CELESTE: A little.

LE GENTIL: I'm glad.

CELESTE: Why?

LE GENTIL: Because I find that I am terrified of you. It's the dress,
                I think.

CELESTE: The dress?

LE GENTIL: The dress, yes, definitely. It's quite elaborate, isn't it?
                Almost like a wedding gown.

CELESTE: It's not at all like a wedding gown.

LE GENTIL: No? Well, what would I know? Where I've been
                women don't bother much with clothes. Some of
                them don't bother with clothes at all. *(He watches her,
                laughs, and moves away.)* I'm glad to see you still know
                how to blush, Celeste.

CELESTE: I wish I didn't.

LE GENTIL: What did you say?

CELESTE: I said I wish I didn't and I hope that soon I won't!

LE GENTIL: There's that candour that I like so much. Thank God
                you haven't lost it. Thank God you look the way you
                do—exactly as I'd hoped. No, better; even better. You
                put me in mind of a ship.

CELESTE: A ship?

LE GENTIL: A particular ship. I'll tell you about her, if you're
                interested. Maybe you're not.

CELESTE: I am.

LE GENTIL: She was called *La Marielle*. You can tell by her name
                what kind of ship she was. *La Marielle!* What a
                beauty—sleek and lithe and limber. There weren't a
                handful of ships on the sea that could leave her

astern. We were somewhere east of the Seychelles.
That's—

CELESTE: Just north of Île de France.

LE GENTIL: You did read my letters. That's a relief. I suppose you
memorized them, too.

CELESTE: *(Turning away.)* Of course not.

LE GENTIL: We were becalmed—had been for days; an eternity, it
seemed. One morning I heard the captain say to the
mate, "Look out for a squall today." I thought he
must be joking. The sea was like a duckpond, not a
cloud in the sky, not enough wind to blow a fly off the
sails. At about mid-day a breeze sprang up; the sea
began to swell and roll. The captain came running.
"All hands on deck! Make fast for a flying squall!"
They went up like a swarm of monkeys, but before
they could finish the job, it was on us—a mountain of
storm. It hit us with such force, it knocked *La Marielle*
clean on her side. I thought we were lost. I did, by
God, I thought for certain we were lost.

CELESTE: You didn't tell me this.

LE GENTIL: But she recovered herself. It took her a second or two
but she did it. She weathered that squall, came
through it as though she were charmed. Because for
all her grace and speed and splendour, she had the
heart of a man o'war. She haunts me, *La Marielle*. I
look for her everywhere. Are you jealous?

CELESTE: Of a ship?

LE GENTIL: It's no joke, Celeste. Could you marry a man who's in
love with a ship?

CELESTE: When you left, you were in love with the sky.

LE GENTIL: I'm still in love with the sky. The sky, the sea, the
tropics. I fall in love quite readily, it seems, but only
with the truly splendid. Are you splendid, Celeste?

CELESTE: I'm afraid not.

LE GENTIL: You look splendid.

CELESTE: Do I?

LE GENTIL: Oh yes, you look like *La Marielle*. But are you like her? If you were knocked flat on your side by a flying squall, would you recover?

CELESTE: But I'm not likely to be, am I.

                He stares at her.

               I don't understand what you're trying to tell me. If you're saying that you don't want to marry me—

LE GENTIL: Of course I want to marry you. My God, haven't I come halfway round the world to do it? But you must understand who I am, Celeste. You must be clear about that. The places I've been—they've changed me. I know, now, how vast the world is, and how beautiful. I believe we're meant to respond to that beauty, not in a miserly fashion but with all the freshness and fullness it deserves. I believe we're meant to live always on the edge of discovery. I don't know if I can explain it in a way you'll understand but something happens, when you get out there, time...dissolves. Weeks, months, days—these things don't exist. Only the moment exists, and the will to live it fully. You feel a little drunk, sometimes—you actually feel quite giddy—on the power of the moment. You feel as though your life is an odyssey, and that to live it less fully than you can would be a travesty. *(Beat; he turns away.)* Listen to me. How can I expect you to understand? How can anyone understand odysseys when all they've known is needlework?

                He moves to the window and stares out.

CELESTE: This may come as a surprise to you, but I don't know the first thing about needlework.

LE GENTIL: No?

CELESTE: No. I don't do it, you see. I don't do any of it. I don't baste, I don't sew, I don't knit, I don't mend, I don't darn, I don't tat, I don't embroider and I do not do petti-point!

He turns to face her.

I do, however, read. And because I can read I can learn. Oh, I can't actually travel—you have the advantage of me there—but I can read about travel, I can dream about it, I can imagine what it's like. I've been everywhere with you. You don't know it, but I have. I know every inch of sea you've sailed, every island you've set foot on. I know how the rains come sweeping across the mountains of Île de France, and how the island itself lies curled in the sea like an oyster. I know about doldrums and trade winds and tides. Tides! Tides are so mysterious. We've known about them since the days of Alexander, yet there's so much we don't know. Why, for instance, there are two high and two low tides every day in some places, and only one in others. Why the tides of Saint-Malo rise almost ten metres and only a fraction of that on the islands you visited. They do; did you know that?

LE GENTIL: No.

CELESTE: I want to know why. I want to know everything there is to know, before I die. This was your gift to me. You pointed me at the sky and said, look! And when I looked, what did I see? Mirrors! Mirrors reflecting mirrors reflecting mirrors, on and on into infinity. So much to know, so much to learn, so much to wonder about. Once you begin to wonder, it's impossible, isn't it—inconceivable!—to abandon that sense of wonder for anything as straightforward and mundane as a needle and a piece of thread.

               Silence.

LE GENTIL: My God, Celeste. I had no idea. *(Suddenly he laughs.)* To think that you would do this! *(He moves to her.)* This is wonderful! I can't tell you how delighted I am, I can't begin to tell you.

CELESTE: I was hoping you'd be pleased.

LE GENTIL: Pleased! There's nothing you could have done that would have pleased me more. This is wonderful. This makes everything possible! Because once you know what it is to wonder, to have that hunger—(*Breaking off, he takes her hands.*) I've travelled half the world, seen such beauty it would stun the mind. But I haven't seen anything, anywhere, as beautiful as you. Will you marry me, Celeste? Immediately? Without reservation?

CELESTE: Yes.

LE GENTIL: Yes! Good. Wonderful. Now. Where would you like me to take you? We're going away together, just the two of us. I want you all to myself from the day I marry you until the day I have to leave. We'll start a family. You wanted to do that before I went away the last time, remember? Well, this time we're going to do it. We'll start a family, and then when I come back—

CELESTE: Leave? You're going to leave? Of course you are, how stupid of me. This is what you've been saying all along!

CELESTE runs toward the exit.

LE GENTIL: Celeste!

He runs after her, and takes hold of her. She struggles to get free.

Stop it. Stop it, Celeste.

She obeys.

Come and sit down. (*Very shaken.*) Please sit down, and I'll explain.

She lets him lead her to a chair, and sinks into it.

I've always suspected there were better places for charting the transit than Pondichéry. I did some calculations, and I found one. It's called Manila.

CELESTE: What does it matter. The transit is over. What does it matter now where the best place was?

LE GENTIL: I'm not talking about the last transit, I'm talking about the next one. The Academy wants someone in Pondichéry, since by the grace of God it happens to be French again, but—

CELESTE: My God.

LE GENTIL: I'm making a bid for Manila. From Manila, a man could sail on to Mexico, down the coast of South America, around Cape Horn and home across the Atlantic. A complete circumnavigation of the globe!

CELESTE: You're going away again. You've just barely walked through the door, and you're going away.

LE GENTIL: Not immediately. Not for months.

CELESTE: How many months?

LE GENTIL: Eight, possibly ten. I intend to spend them all with you.

CELESTE: How long this time?

LE GENTIL: How long will I be gone? Three years.

                CELESTE laughs.

                I swear to you, Celeste, on everything that's holy: three years, no more.

CELESTE: What if you miss it?

LE GENTIL: The transit? I won't.

CELESTE: You missed the last one.

LE GENTIL: That was because of the war. There's no war now, thank God.

CELESTE: What if it's cloudy?

LE GENTIL: That's unlikely, in Manila; that's the point.

CELESTE: What if it is? You'll be going back to chart the next one.

LE GENTIL: Definitely not.

CELESTE: You say that now.

LE GENTIL: There won't be another transit of Venus for more than a hundred years.

CELESTE: And you'd let that stop you?!

LE GENTIL: *(Beat.)* Try to understand, Celeste—

CELESTE: This will be the end of me.

LE GENTIL: No, it won't. You'll ride right through it. You'll ride right through it and come out stronger, and more splendid, on the other side.

CELESTE: Oh! I see.

LE GENTIL: I know you have it in you. I'm counting on that.

CELESTE: I'm not a ship.

LE GENTIL: You know what I mean.

CELESTE: I'm not a bloody ship!

LE GENTIL: Please try to understand. I chose to serve God in a different way. But I haven't done it yet, I haven't done what I was meant to do. All I want—all I want, Celeste—is the chance to pull a single slender thread from the veil of ignorance we wear, that clouds our understanding of the universe, and of God. If God intended to deny me this work, why would He have allowed me to watch the first transit? Why take me all that way, only to strand me on a ship at sea where I could watch the transit but not measure it? There had to be a reason, and this is what it was: to ensure that I'd go back to chart the next one.

CELESTE: You can't be certain that's the reason.

LE GENTIL:	I am. I am certain. I searched for that reason for a long, long time, and finally I understood. It's my life's work, Celeste. Everything I've learned and seen and done has been a kind of preparation for it. I'm suited to it, body, mind, and soul. This is what I mean about the will to live life fully. I have that will, and I have it for it purpose.
CELESTE:	*(Beat.)* Does Demarais know about this?
LE GENTIL:	He knew I was considering it.
CELESTE:	Of course! He's not going with you, though.
LE GENTIL:	He shouldn't have come with me the first time.
CELESTE:	Then take me. Le Gentil? Take me with you when you go.
LE GENTIL:	Come, Celeste—
CELESTE:	I won't be any trouble. I've studied all of it. I know about the seas, and sailing. I know about the stars. You can teach me to assist you. I can help.

LE GENTIL stands.

LE GENTIL:	Absolutely not. It's dangerous, it's unhealthy. Look at Demarais.
CELESTE:	Look at you.
LE GENTIL:	No. Definitely not. I'd never risk it.
CELESTE:	Don't leave me. Don't go off and leave me again, Le Gentil—
LE GENTIL:	For the love of Christ, stop calling me Le Gentil! My God, if you're going to marry me, isn't it time for something a little less impersonal?

Pause.

CELESTE:	There'll be no marriage.
LE GENTIL:	You don't mean that.

CELESTE: I do.

LE GENTIL: You're only saying it because you're upset.

CELESTE: I need you, Guillaume. I don't know if you understand what that means, but I need you. I'm sick to death of making do with dreams, and letters—and a phantom lover. I want a real lover! I want a husband, I want a family, I want a future. I don't want to be stuck on a shelf, like a book nobody bothers to read. I want to get started... with my life! My life is an odyssey, too. Why must it be played out on such a tiny map?

LE GENTIL: What would you have me do, stay home and grow miserable? Difficult to live with, impossible to please? Useless and idle?

CELESTE: You wouldn't have to be idle. You could find something to do.

LE GENTIL: Such as?

CELESTE: You could write your memoirs.

LE GENTIL: That's for old men.

CELESTE: You could—

LE GENTIL: I'm forty-one, Celeste. I'm strong and healthy. I still need what's difficult, to try my hand at, not what's easy. I need an idea in my mind large enough to scare the hell out of me. That's the only way I can function.

CELESTE: Don't leave me. I'm begging you—

LE GENTIL: Don't. Don't ever beg. I won't compromise, Celeste—

CELESTE: Neither will I.

LE GENTIL: I'm warning you. If you persist in this foolishness, I won't linger here, trying to change your mind. I'll leave immediately.

CELESTE: Perhaps you should.

LE GENTIL: I can, quite easily. I can get a ship within a fortnight. I can be back in the tropics by Christmas.

CELESTE: That should make you very happy.

LE GENTIL: It will, believe me!

CELESTE: Then what are you waiting for? Do it! Do it, Guillaume. It will be easier for everyone.

                        CELESTE turns abruptly and moves toward the exit. He stops her with a voice like thunder.

LE GENTIL: Don't you dare walk out of here like this!

                        She stops moving.

                        Don't you dare do this! Don't—ask me—to choose! I can't choose. I wish my work were here. It's not. I wish I could take you with me. I can't. For your sake, I wish I were another kind of man. But would you love me if I were? Would you? *(Beat.)* I need to be able to count on you, Celeste. I need to be able to dream about you while I'm gone. If you won't marry me now, at least tell me you'll wait. Tell me you'll wait, Celeste.

CELESTE: How did this happen? I don't understand! Of the dream that was my life, this is the nightmare.

LE GENTIL: If I go back immediately, I can save time on the other end. I can arrange to leave for home right after the transit. Will you wait for me, if I can do that? Will you?

CELESTE: How do I know you'll ever want to stay? How do I even know you'll come back?

LE GENTIL: I'll come back. I will, Celeste. Because you and I—you and I are fixed by God in a kind of orbit. I circle round you like a planet around the sun. No matter how far I wander, you always draw me back. You always do, Celeste. You always do.

                        Pause.

CELESTE: There'll be no excuses this time. No delays. Once the transit is over, you must come straight home. I'll be waiting for you, but only on that condition. I won't go on forever, competing with the universe. I won't do it.

                She exits.

                Blackout.

                End of Act Two.

Act Three

The sitting room. Afternoon; a pale wintry day. Everything is covered in sheets. LE GENTIL, wearing an overcoat, stands at a window. He has set down a well-worn valise somewhere in the room. In one hand he holds a small gift. To the extent possible, he should appear much older than in Act Two. Suddenly, MARGOT runs on, in a coat and hat.

MARGOT: Guillaume? Is it really you? What a shock you've given us! I didn't know whether to laugh or cry, when I got your note. I hardly dared believe it. Guillaume?

LE GENTIL: Where is she?

MARGOT: I beg your pardon?

LE GENTIL: Celeste, where is she?

MARGOT: I couldn't simply leave a message; you have to understand. I felt I had to speak to her in person. That's why I'm a little late, I—

LE GENTIL: She's coming, then.

MARGOT: I was interrupted again and again as I came through. You can't imagine the sensation you've caused. People kept running to their windows, crying, "Is it true, is it really true?" They're saying you've been raised from the dead. Like Lazarus!

LE GENTIL: But is she coming, Margot?

MARGOT: I'm not sure.

LE GENTIL: What does that mean?

MARGOT: Please. Try to understand the position you've put her in. It's not an easy thing, to face the dead. I'm sure— I'm sure she'll find the strength to do what's right. You mustn't be impatient. The news is still so fresh.

LE GENTIL: Is she married? Is she married, yes or no?

MARGOT: No.

LE GENTIL: No! God be thanked. She's not ill?

MARGOT: No.

LE GENTIL: That's all I ask.

                        MARGOT shudders.

MARGOT: My goodness, the house is cold. It feels as though it's been closed up forever. Oh, Guillaume. Just look at you! You look as though you truly have been raised from the dead.

LE GENTIL: Nonsense.

                        He moves away from the window.

                I'm a little tired from travel, nothing more. I had to come across the Pyrenees by goat-cart, if you can picture it.

MARGOT: Goat-cart?

LE GENTIL: Anything was preferable to the sea. Come and sit down, Margot, please.

                        MARGOT obeys. He sits across from her.

                I've just come from my solicitor. My former solicitor, I should say; naturally, I dismissed him. He tells me that my mother has been sent away.

MARGOT: She's with her cousin in Lyon. We had no choice, you see. Once they decided that you must be dead—

LE GENTIL: I want you to go and bring her back.

MARGOT:	When?
LE GENTIL:	Immediately. Tomorrow.
MARGOT:	Guillaume, I have another position now. I can't simply—
LE GENTIL:	Give it up.
MARGOT:	Give it up! Just like that?
LE GENTIL:	Yes. You belong here, Margot. This is your home. If you like, I'll send a note to your employer. I'll tell him I've been raised from the dead; that ought to inspire him to oblige.
MARGOT:	I'm afraid it's not that simple.
LE GENTIL:	Margot, please! I am trying to put my life back together. Don't impede me.
MARGOT:	*(Controlling herself with an effort.)* Your life, Guillaume—your life is only one of several which have been quite drastically upset. You can't come walking in here after all this time and start demanding things. And expect us all to fall in line!
LE GENTIL:	Please try to understand. I've spent twenty-nine months trying to get home—twenty-nine months!— and everything has gone against me. And now— now, when I'm finally able to stand under my own roof—*(With a gesture that takes in the room.)*—look at it! Just look at it! In my worst nightmares, I never imagined I'd be coming back to this.
MARGOT:	How did it happen, Guillaume, that we didn't hear from you? The last letter Celeste has arrived a full two years ago.
LE GENTIL:	For a time I couldn't write. I was ill.
MARGOT:	Ill.
LE GENTIL:	I was flat on my back for eight solid months. Couldn't find the strength to sit, let alone to write. Couldn't get out of India to save my soul! And when I did, when I

finally got as far as Île de France, it was only to fall ill again. Eventually, when I was well enough at last to go on, every ship I set foot on carried me into some fresh tragedy. One of them actually carried me into a hurricane. What an experience that was! I tried again and again to get away, set out in half a dozen ships; again and again I failed. If anyone had told me a few years ago that the day would come when the sight of the sea would make me want to weep—*(He breaks off.)*

MARGOT: But why didn't you let her know, Guillaume? One letter! One letter, to say you were alive.

LE GENTIL: It's difficult to explain, I was confused. I couldn't seem to find the will.

MARGOT: You made a promise to Celeste. You broke that promise, and you didn't tell her why. You simply disappeared! It was as though the sea had opened up and swallowed you whole. And now you come along, at this late date, and tell me that you couldn't seem to find the will!

            Pause.

LE GENTIL: I was ashamed. I used to know what I was meant to do. I was meant to unravel God's great mysteries! But I was wrong. Sometimes, Margot...sometimes I still feel quite confused. I don't mean up here—*(He taps his forehead.)*—I mean—*(Taps his chest.)* I look back, and search my life, and it seems to me that in my confidence, in my supreme self-confidence, all I've brought to everyone I've loved, and been loved by, is pain. What a legacy! Clearly, I must set things right. But I don't—you see, this is the worst of it. I don't know if I'll ever be able to trust my judgement again.

MARGOT: Now listen to me, Guillaume. You've been very ill, you've had a long journey, you're exhausted. You must try not to dwell on these things. Once you've had a chance to recover your strength, you'll find your optimism will return as well.

LE GENTIL: You're very kind, Margot. Much kinder than I

deserve. *(Not meeting her eyes.)* I'm afraid there was a time I caused you pain, as well.

MARGOT: If I denied that, I'd be denying that I ever cared for you. And that would be a lie. I did care for you once, but I cared much more for Celeste.

He stares gloomily at his hands.

LE GENTIL: I often thought of Demarais, while I was ill. I've been wanting to ask about him. Something tells me it hasn't gone well for him.

MARGOT: No.

LE GENTIL: My God.

MARGOT: I'm afraid—

LE GENTIL: No, don't tell me. There's only so much bad news a man can stomach in a day. *(He stands and moves away.)* You're right, you know. The house is cold. I've just begun to feel it.

MARGOT: Where will you stay tonight?

LE GENTIL: Here, of course.

MARGOT: In this empty house? No heat, no food—

LE GENTIL: I don't need either.

MARGOT: On the contrary, you need both, especially when you've been so ill. I was going to suggest—

LE GENTIL: I'm staying here.

MARGOT: For heaven's sake!

LE GENTIL: I want my home restored to me. I want everything as it was, exactly. You'll fetch my mother home tomorrow. If you need a letter, I will write one. In fact, I'll write it now.

LE GENTIL moves to the valise, opens it, and takes out writing materials.

MARGOT:	Guillaume. You've been gone a very long time. You can't simply reappear suddenly, out of the blue—and expect everything to be the way it was.
LE GENTIL:	Not immediately, perhaps, but I can make a start.
MARGOT:	I'm afraid things may be a little more complicated than you realize.
LE GENTIL:	Complicated! You sound like my solicitor. He's gone and sold off half the property—to pay my debts, he says. Debts! I've never been in debt in my life. People I haven't even heard of have laid claim to my estate. And then, as if all this weren't bad enough, there's my colleagues at the Academy. They've given away my seat, for God's sake. After all the work I've done! This would never have happened if Delisle were alive. He would never...

He leans on the desk for support. MARGOT stands.

MARGOT:	What's the matter?

He waves her away.

LE GENTIL:	Nothing.
MAARGOT:	You don't look well at all.
LE GENTIL:	I'm fine. fine! *(Sinking into a chair.)* To whom do I address this?
MARGOT:	There's no point in writing that now.
LE GENTIL:	Why not?
MARGOT:	I'll get it later, if I need it. If I decide to fetch your mother.
LE GENTIL:	If you decide—?
MARGOT:	I think you should prepare yourself, Guillaume. As many disappointments as you've had today, you should prepare yourself for more.

CELESTE enters quietly, wearing a cloak or cape.

Le GENTIL: I know my mother's mind is gone. I know that. She needs attention night and day; that I know as well. I intend to see that she—

He breaks off; he has seen CELESTE. He stares at her.

How do you do that? How do you manage to grow more and more beautiful while the rest of the world—grows gray? Celeste?

He stands and moves towards CELESTE, but something in her attitude discourages him. He stops.

I'm glad you've come. Your mother wasn't sure you'd do it. I knew you would, though I realize it's been a shock for you to discover I'm alive. It's been a shock for me to discover I've been dead! Celeste?

MARGOT: Why don't you sit down, Celeste?

CELESTE: I dreamt this, all of it. I dreamt it over and over. Long after they said that you were dead, long after I'd forced myself to believe it, I dreamt you were alive, and had come back to me—just like this! And I stood here, staring at you. And I couldn't speak for pain.

MARGOT: Celeste.

CELESTE: I couldn't understand; it made no sense. Why not joy instead of pain? It was terrible; it always woke me up. And then I'd remember that you were dead, and none of it was true. It was an invention of the mind, echoing the agony of the heart. It was never meant to be true.

MARGOT: *(Moving to her.)* Come and sit down.

CELESTE: No. I can't stay.

MARGOT: I have to leave myself, quite soon. We'll walk back together.

CELESTE allows MARGOT to lead her to a chair. She sits. MARGOT starts off.

CELESTE: *(To MARGOT.)* Where are you going?

MARGOT: To lay out some blankets.

CELESTE: No, Mother—

MARGOT: He insists on staying here, and the house is very cold.

CELESTE: I need you here!

MARGOT: I know. I won't be long.

LE GENTIL: *(To MARGOT.)* Is she all right?

MARGOT: She will be. Go gently with her, please.

                MARGOT exits. Beat.

LE GENTIL: My God, Celeste, I'm sorry. It didn't occur to me
                they'd take it into their heads to declare me dead. I
                hope you understand that. If I'd known they'd done
                that, I'd have... I don't know what I would have
                done.

CELESTE: Well, it doesn't matter now.

LE GENTIL: You're sure?

CELESTE: I have what I want.

LE GENTIL: *(Unable to help himself.)* You look so beautiful! Just to
                look at you makes me feel thirty-five again.

                She turns away. He adopts a lighter tone.

                What have you been doing, to become so beautiful?

CELESTE: What do you mean?

LE GENTIL: Nothing, I only—well, for instance, do you still like to
                read?

CELESTE: Not as much.

LE GENTIL: You're not still fascinated with the tides?

CELESTE: Not really.

LE GENTIL: What do you do then, with your time?

CELESTE:	*(Smiles.)* Needlework.
LE GENTIL:	*(Grins.)* Seriously, now.
CELESTE:	*(Seriously.)* Needlework.

He has no idea what to make of this. He remembers the gift in his hand.

LE GENTIL: I have a gift for you, Celeste. I hope you'll accept it. *(Again, striving for lightness.)* If not, I'll have to give them to some other woman, and I don't know any who could wear them as well as you.

He offers her the package. She stares at it but doesn't take it.

Combs, for your hair. Tortoise-shell. Very beautiful, I think. From the Celebes.

CELESTE: I'm sorry. I don't wear combs.

LE GENTIL: *(Beat.)* Well, I—have other gifts. In fact, I have a chest full but it hasn't yet arrived. I sent it on by ship from Cadiz. Silks and cottons; fine lace and spices. Fans, jewels, carvings.

CELESTE: It's odd, isn't it, to be sitting here? I didn't expect to see this room again. Your mother would be so impressed! With your escape. From the deep. We thought you'd drowned.

LE GENTIL: I know.

CELESTE: We saw you lying at the bottom of the sea, your bones picked clean long since by little fish. We found it easier to think of you that way. We had a lot in common, your mother and I.

LE GENTIL: I'm going to bring her home, Celeste, as soon as possible. Look after her—

CELESTE: We grieved you together, the three of us. Your mother, my mother, and I. Never was a man so well-wept!

He sits next to her.

LE GENTIL: I wanted to get home, Celeste. More than anything in the world, I wanted to get home to you. I'd have walked the oceans, if I could have.

CELESTE: No, don't say this. I don't want any explanations.

LE GENTIL: You have to let me explain—

CELESTE: No. I don't have to. And if you insist, I will leave immediately.

LE GENTIL: Celeste, for pity's sake—

CELESTE: *(To finish it.)* You got your measurements; what else matters?

LE GENTIL: I—

CELESTE: I knew you would, even from Pondichéry. If it was ever cloudy there, you didn't mention it. *(Quoting from memory.)* "The nights here are of the greatest beauty. You cannot imagine how stunning is the sky that falls around me on these perfect, scented nights." You remember that, I'm sure. *(Again from memory.)* "Today the wind is from the southeast, a good omen. This wind is called the broom of the coast, and always brings serenity." That was early on the morning of the transit. So you got your measurements, all right, but you weren't ready to come home—*(She starts to lose control.)*—for whatever reason—

LE GENTIL: Celeste—

CELESTE: That's why the letters stopped. And if that's not true, then I don't want to know the truth.

LE GENTIL: In all these months, I have been engaged in a kind of struggle—with myself, and also, in a way, with God. I thought, you see—I always believed—that God had hidden His most precious secrets where they would be most difficult to find. I would look at the sky, or the sea—

CELESTE: I don't want to hear this.

LE GENTIL: And know that there the challenge lay. It didn't occur to me to look elsewhere—

CELESTE: I don't want to hear this!

LE GENTIL: It didn't occur to me that perhaps He had created all those things for another reason—

CELESTE: I don't want to know anything! I have it all constructed in my mind, and I won't allow you to get in there again and tear it down. I won't allow it!

LE GENTIL: I'm to be condemned without a trial, is that it? Even the worst of criminals—

MARGOT enters.

MARGOT: There, that's done. Did I interrupt?

LE GENTIL: Yes!

CELESTE: No! *(To MARGOT.)* We have nothing to say that can't be said in front of you. Is that not so, Guillaume?

LE GENTIL: I don't wish to be rude, but—

CELESTE: *(To MARGOT.)* There, you see? He doesn't wish to be rude.

LE GENTIL: Celeste, we have so much to say to one another, so much to talk about. I want to get to know you again. I want to know if you still dream of me. Do you, Celeste?

CELESTE: I see you at the bottom of the sea—a skull with gaping holes where the eyes once hung, a space inside the skull so vast and inhospitable no thought can linger there. No thought of any kind: of Venus, or of India; of the sky, or ships, or tides; and certainly no thought of me. I like that. I like to think of all that space within your skull and nothing flowing through it but the sea.

Again, LE GENTIL is stunned into silence.

LE GENTIL: What kind of talk is this?!

MARGOT: Try to understand. She's been through so much.

LE GENTIL: I have not come ten thousand leagues, with death clinging to my coattails, to listen to talk like this! What do you expect me to do, for God's sake, apologize for staying alive?

MARGOT: Of course not.

LE GENTIL: Celeste?

She faces him.

CELESTE: I don't know what your plans are, or your expectations—

LE GENTIL: The hell you don't.

CELESTE: The reason I've come here... is to tell you that I'm going to have a child. I'm very happy about this, and I hope you'll do me the great courtesy of being happy for me.

Silence; it seems to go on forever.

LE GENTIL: Whose child? Whose—child are you expecting?

CELESTE: Does it matter?

LE GENTIL: For the love of Christ!

CELESTE: I don't believe it matters.

LE GENTIL: You don't believe it matters! It looks as though it's the father who doesn't believe it matters.

CELESTE: Nothing could be farther from the truth.

LE GENTIL: Well, where is he, then? Doesn't he know where his duty lies? What kind of man is this?

CELESTE: A gentle man.

LE GENTIL: A gentleman! He's no gentleman. If that was my child in your belly, if I was its father—

CELESTE: But it isn't. And you aren't.

A stand-off. Pause.

LE GENTIL: I want to meet the father.

CELESTE: No.

LE GENTIL: I insist on meeting him!

CELESTE: It's not possible.

LE GENTIL: Why not?

MARGOT: The father is dead. He intended to marry Celeste, but she delayed. And now he's dead.

LE GENTIL: That sounds like a story to me.

MARGOT: Guillaume!

LE GENTIL: It sounds like the sort of story people invent to protect the honour of a woman who has none.

CELESTE: That's right, I have no honour. Thank God for that. I never much liked it, anyway.

LE GENTIL: I know that well enough. You were always trying to give it away.

CELESTE: All I needed was a man who cared enough to take it!

MARGOT: Stop it, both of you! You're not going to tear each other into little pieces, not in my presence. Do you understand? Now. I want you to sit down, Celeste.

CELESTE: No. I'm going to leave.

MARGOT: You are going to sit down and you are going to do it now.

                CELESTE obeys. MARGOT turns to LE GENTIL.

               I understand how difficult this is for you. But you must remember that in her condition—

LE GENTIL: I'm sorry.

MARGOT: Your very presence is a shock to her. I can't allow you to go on this way. If you persist, I'll take Celeste away from here immediately. Do you understand?

LE GENTIL: Of course.

Pause. LE GENTIL turns to CELESTE.

Please forgive me. I had no right to say that.

CELESTE: It's I who should apologize. I'm sure there was a better way to tell you, but for the life of me I couldn't think of it.

LE GENTIL: When is the baby due, Celeste?

CELESTE: April.

LE GENTIL: And what are your plans? How will you support your child?

CELESTE: I have a little money now, left me by the father—

LE GENTIL: A *little* money.

CELESTE: Enough.

He takes a step towards her.

LE GENTIL: Listen, Celeste—

CELESTE: I'm going to emigrate. To New France.

LE GENTIL: New France! You can't be serious.

CELESTE: I am. As soon as the child is old enough to travel.

LE GENTIL: *(An appeal.)* Margot?

MARGOT: If she goes, I intend to go with her.

LE GENTIL: *(To CELESTE.)* And what do you expect to do, in that wilderness?

CELESTE: Begin my life. I hope to get a position as a governess, perhaps even as a teacher. It's a rough place, but it has a future. And I want my child to have a future.

He moves to her.

LE GENTIL: Listen to me, Celeste. These plans of yours, they may have been necessary when you thought that I was dead. They're not necessary now. I want to marry you. I don't care who the father is, don't care if he's alive or dead; it's irrelevant. I'm asking you, in all humility, to be my wife. After all this time, it still gives me more pleasure to look at you than at anything else in the world.

CELESTE: *(fighting back tears.)* Do you see, Mother? See how it is? What are you going to do with a man like this? This man! This man never learns when to come and when to go and when to simply—stay away!

LE GENTIL: Tell me you'll marry me, Celeste.

CELESTE: It's too late.

LE GENTIL: No, it's not too late. I won't accept that. I won't allow you to do this. I will not allow you to throw away your future, and mine as well, because of one fateful indiscretion.

CELESTE: One—? No, you don't understand.

MARGOT: Let it go, Celeste.

CELESTE: I grieved you, Guillaume. From the moment I understood that you would break your promise, long before they said that you were dead, I grieved you! If rooms could talk, these rooms would tell... how much I grieved. *(Beat.)* At first I went to him—simply to talk about you. He'd been with you through so much, he knew you so well. It was almost as though by touching him I could reach you. Then one day I looked at him and everything had changed. I realized I wasn't grieving anymore. Somewhere along the way, the thing I never thought was possible had happened: I'd stopped loving you. It wasn't you I wanted to be close to, it was him. Because it gave me so much joy! And I didn't just love him a little bit; I loved him with everything I had. I loved him—the way I'd wanted to love you. I had him for seven months. Seven months! It seems to be my fate to fall in love with men who go away.

LE GENTIL sinks into a chair.

MARGOT: *(To LE GENTIL.)* He caught pneumonia a few months ago. He'd had so many relapses; each one left him weaker than the last.

CELESTE: You did what you were meant to do. You came into the world and looked around—with your bright, impressionable eye! You chose the most exciting thing you could imagine doing, and you did it. You let the beauty of the world, and all its mysteries, touch you and transform you. You kept an open heart. For all those things, I loved you. But I don't love you now, and I never could again. And I can't pity you.

CELESTE exits. Silence.

LE GENTIL: I never believed I'd lose her. When I missed the first transit, even after I missed the second, she was always there. She shone for me, in the distance, like the sun.

MARGOT: You missed the second transit? Oh, Guillaume! And we assumed all along...

LE GENTIL: I heard the sand-bar moaning from the southeast, early on the morning of the transit. This made me think the wind was still from that direction. I was elated. This wind is called the broom of the gods, and it always—*(Breaking off.)* Did I say the gods? I meant the coast. It's called the broom of the coast, and it always brings serenity. But I was wrong. The wind had changed. The sky was covered everywhere in cloud. And in Manila, where I could have been if I'd had my way, the skies were perfectly clear.

MARGOT doesn't know what to say. Finally, she moves to him.

MARGOT: I have to go, Guillaume—to see that she gets safely home. There are beggars everywhere these days, and they seem to prey on women. Guillaume?

No response. MARGOT hesitates, torn between staying and going. Finally, she exits. LE GENTIL sits motionless for a very long time. Then he stands or turns. In doing so, he accidentally pulls a sheet from a piece of furniture; he discovers the furniture is covered in needlework. He removes another sheet; more needlework. He moves from room to room, removing sheets. To his astonishment, everything he uncovers is draped in or decorated with some form of needlework. He understands that all this needlework is the physical manifestation of CELESTE's grief for him. Finally, he sinks back into a chair.

Blackout.

The End.